THE FALL OF ROME

Second Edition

THE
FALL OF ROME
Can It Be Explained?

Edited by MORTIMER CHAMBERS
University of California, Los Angeles

HOLT, RINEHART AND WINSTON
New York • Chicago • San Francisco • Atlanta
Dallas • Montreal • Toronto • London • Sydney

Cover illustration: Romans battling Gauls. Detail from a
sarcophagus (A.D. 150–160) in the Capitoline Museum,
Rome. *(Alinari)*

Copyright © 1963, 1970 by Holt, Rinehart and Winston, Inc.
All Rights Reserved
Library of Congress Catalog Card Number: 75–135290

ISBN: 0-03-084478-9

Printed in the United States of America
123 008 987

CONTENTS

The Roman Forum, looking toward the Colosseum. (*Pan American Airways*)

INTRODUCTION

History-writing is *explanation*. That alone distinguishes it from the mere collecting of facts, accurately dated and lucidly described, in the form of chronicles. The difference between a "historian" and a "chronicler"—between, let us say, Thucydides and Livy in ancient historiography—is commonly attributed to the historian's deeper inquiry into causation, into the progress and change of events, and into the question *Why?* Yet the historian brings to this work no specially superior intellectual equipment. His explanations are based in part on the same kind of intuition, prejudice, and calculation that we all use in explaining such ordinary events as the actions of our friends or the success or failure of our enterprises. The historian will try to eliminate subjectivity, hazy terminology, and emotion from his thought; and to the degree that he also gains through research a wider knowledge of all relevant data than a contemporary can amass, he may work his way closer to the real causes of historical events. But if we are ever complacent enough to consider our explanations the only true ones, we may well recall that the subject of this book—the so-called fall of Rome—has tenaciously resisted explanation for centuries.

And this is puzzling. Human history shows no more brilliant example of success in statesmanship than the Roman Empire. It united the entire civilized portion of the West, from Scotland to Egypt, from Gibraltar to Armenia, under a single dominion for more than two centuries. This achievement has never been approached by any later state. The passing of this colossal empire must rank as one of the greatest historical turning points in man's long story. The fall was foreseen and recorded by contemporaries; and within the age of modern historical research, dozens of learned scholars have attacked the problem from their several points of view. For all that, the cause may still elude us. The purpose of this book is to present a collection of several leading explanations for the fall of Rome. The reader must decide for himself how much of the truth any or all of them contain.

We must first know precisely what we are trying to explain. The fall of Rome is traditionally dated to 476 A.D., when the Scirian warlord Odovacar (less properly, Odoacer) forced the abdication of the last Emperor, Augustulus. This date had become canonized as early as the sixth century, when we find chroniclers such as Marcellinus Comes recording under 476:

> Odoacer, the king of the Goths, seized Rome; he condemned Augustulus, the son of Orestes, to exile in the castle of Lucullus in Campania. The Western Empire of the Roman People, which the first of the Augusti, Octavianus Augustus, began to rule in the seven hundred and ninth year after the founding of Rome, ended with this Augustulus.[1]

The year 476 for the fall of Rome was accepted in modern times by Edward Gibbon, who originally ended his *Decline and Fall* at that point. In fact, however, it is highly doubtful that most subjects of the Empire felt any real shock or had to make any deep adjustment in their lives because one dynast in Rome had replaced another. It must have been a long time indeed before this news reached the far corners of Spain or Gaul, nor would it have mattered much to a farmer or craftsman there. J. B. Bury also shows, in the second excerpt reprinted here, that, even if we choose to play the historian's game and fix the end of the Empire, 476 may not be the right date after all. His forceful objections to the date given by the chroniclers and accepted by Gibbon deserve study, even though 476 is unlikely to be displaced in textbooks or popular tradition.

Gibbon also failed to attend to the historical movement that really demands explanation. In the general observations on the fall that he added to his chapter 38—the end of his whole work as he originally planned it—he chose for some reason not to look deeply for the causes of the decline of the Empire. "The story of its ruin" was "simple and obvious," the main cause being attacks by Eurasian barbarians. But to say that the Empire fell because it was overwhelmed by barbarians is scarcely a profound explanation. It also suggests, wrongly, that our main problem is to account for the events of 476.

In fact, 476 was like many another historical turning point: it was a logical, if not an inevitable, conclusion to a long series of connected events. Thoughtful men had observed an apparent decline some time before this. The historian Ammianus Marcellinus, writing after the serious Roman defeat at Adrianople in 378, pointed in a long and rhetorical passage (book 14, chapter 6) to the moral decadence of contemporary Romans. He hoped to explain in this fashion the obvious difficulties of the late fourth century, which were partly responsible for the later division of the Empire into Eastern and Western parts in 395. But a military defeat in the Balkans may have no connection with immorality practiced by nobles or paupers in Rome; and a severe censor could probably have written such a denunciation against the Rome of the Republic, when Caesar (no strict moralist, surely) planted Roman sovereignty in the area of modern France.

Perhaps two decades later than Ammianus, St. Augustine also confronted

[1] *Chronica Minora,* ed. Th. Mommsen (Berlin, 1894), p. 91.

the probable decline of Rome, which had recently been captured and sacked by Alaric in 410. In the opening pages of his *City of God*, Augustine sought to repel the argument that the troubles of the Empire were due to the practice of Christianity, an accusation apparently lodged by some anti-Christians. Gibbon himself was to take up this argument and hold the divisive and weakening effects of Christianity partly responsible for the fall; the same case has been argued in more absurd form by some modern writers. Augustine himself put forth no trenchant historical explanation; but the point to grasp is that he too could and did observe this frightening movement in world affairs.

Among Augustine's successors in the inquiry, the French philosopher Montesquieu deserves mention as a forerunner of Gibbon. In 1734 he published his *Considérations sur les causes de la grandeur des Romains et de leur décadence*. This book is still reprinted from time to time, although its analyses are supported by little detailed scholarship and its generalizations are interesting mainly as specimens of the eighteenth-century approach to historical problems by means of unaided reason. His remark that the laws of Rome lost their force when the state developed into an empire at least touches an important point but would need considerable expansion to be called a major discovery.

The twentieth century has contributed a good many theories on the causes for the fall. A full collection of these lies beyond our scope. But certain kinds of inquiry recur again and again in the literature, and this book assembles representative points of view in which one or another kind of evidence is examined. For instance, did the population of the Empire change for the worse, either in number or in quality? If it could be shown that the Romans and their subjects simply had not enough men to resist the hordes of barbarians on the frontiers, then a large—perhaps the largest— factor in the fall would be identified. Such an argument is advanced by A. E. R. Boak, who attempted to use the methods of demography to show that the population of the Western Empire was seriously diminished by a plague in the second century. Even though Boak stated that he did not believe in any "single major cause" of the collapse of the Western Empire, his whole book is a strong invitation to consider shrinkage of population as one of the most important of whatever causes we finally admit.

But can a decline in population really be proved? We shall always remain undersupplied with statistics of population in antiquity; therefore some use of modern analogy may well be essential in approaching this problem. But Boak's point of view is strongly resisted by M. I. Finley, who comprehensively denies that the evidence supports the conclusions drawn. After reading this critique, the reader should try to decide tentatively to what degree the modern analogies can be relied on.

From a different point of view, E. T. Salmon suggests that the action of the Emperor Caracalla, who bestowed Roman citizenship on nearly all free men living within the Empire in 212, actually had an unforeseen and dangerous result. Men who joined the army with the aim of winning Roman citizenship through service were no longer incited to enlist by this presumably strong motivation. Roman citizenship was worth serving for, since it conferred on a man the right to go to court and to make a legal will, not to speak of its social and other advantages. If it could be acquired automatically, this possibility could have discouraged enlistment by noncitizens.

A factor difficult to assess accurately is the degree to which a man's effectiveness as a soldier or citizen was determined by his "racial" background, the term as it is used here meaning, generally, ethnic groups. But before this question can seem relevant to the fall, it must be shown that the population of the Empire suffered a change in racial composition. The attempt of Tenney Frank to do so was based on a laborious examination of Latin inscriptions in which non-Italian names seem to be profusely recorded. Frank concluded that, because of intermarriage with slaves, "perhaps ninety per cent" of the common people of Rome were partly or wholly descended from Eastern races (that is, from Greece and the Near East).

One of the by-products of the inspiring development of the natural sciences in the last two centuries has been an attempt to apply scientific methods in history; and no one doubts that the writing of history is improved by seeking higher standards of objectivity and thoroughness. But the final aim of some theorists has been to show that historical events conform to laws as effective and inexorable as the laws of science; the true work of the historian would then be to discover and expound these laws. Among such writers, the decline of any political system is explained by appeal to the workings of laws or forces over which man has little control.

The history of technology has been invoked. There has long been a theory that the Roman upper class contributed to its own extinction by taking diluted lead constantly into its diet. S. Colum Gilfillan has done extensive research into this hypothesis and has concluded that the creative elite destroyed itself through lead poisoning. This would not disastrously lower the total population of the Empire, for only a minority of citizens could afford lead pipes and cooking ware. Whatever validity this particular theory may have, it is indeed strange that the Roman aristocracy, with access to the most expensive diet and the most comfortable housing, could not reproduce itself beyond the first century A.D. The British aristocracy, and the endless stream of Adamses and Cabots in America, are an almost incomprehensible contrast with the short-lived noble families of imperial Rome.

The validity of economic arguments is seriously questioned by the great Russian historian M. I. Rostovtzeff, who had already presented his own view of the fall. In his monumental *Social and Economic History of the Roman Empire* (1926; 2d English ed., 1957) his explanation was not economic but social. The Empire collapsed because of a dislocation in its class structure: "Is not every civilization bound to decay as soon as it begins to penetrate the masses?" An incisive criticism of Rostovtzeff's doctrine was made by Meyer Reinhold. His major point is that the ancient world did not have "classes" in the modern sense; thus an assumed struggle between large, powerful classes is simply not appropriate to the social structure of antiquity. Another kind of political explanation is put forth by F. W. Walbank: the overorganized and tightly controlled Empire subjected the weak to such an extreme degree of compulsion that all initiative and fighting spirit were crushed. Although his description of the "corporative state" is a vivid one, we may still conjecture that even a people under political compulsion might have been able to keep the barbarians from crossing the frontiers. The political structure of the Empire alone does not wholly account for its fall, nor did Walbank make such an assertion.

But did the Empire actually fall? Long ago Montesquieu pointed to a fact that must be kept before us at all times. When we speak of the fall of Rome, we must remember that this term can be applied only to the Western Empire. The Eastern, or Byzantine, Empire certainly did not fall in 476 and in fact continued for nearly another thousand years until the capture of Constantinople in 1453. Therefore any explanation for the fall must show why the Eastern Empire avoided the fate of the Western one. This dilemma has raised difficulties for more than one of the sometimes extravagant suggestions put forth in modern times. Some of the excerpts collected in this book may be vulnerable to the objection that they do not expose those conditions that led to a decline in the West while leaving the East comparatively vigorous. These observations were restated in a timely warning by the great Byzantine historian Norman Baynes. After a review of some of his predecessors' theories, he suggested that the survival of the East was due to its greater reserves in wealth and manpower; the West was more damagingly attacked by the barbarians. Perhaps this argument rests partly on one already mentioned; for if the East had superior manpower, then manpower shortage in the West immediately arises as a factor to be considered.

Thus one argument leads into another, and it continues to be difficult to sustain any single theory as the only possible explanation for the massive historical change under consideration. The contemporary British historian A. H. M. Jones, confronting the problem at the end of his erudite *The Later Roman Empire*, was drawn to look once more at the political and military aspects of the decline. In a way, Jones returns to the approach taken by Gibbon—no matter what were the contributing economic or demographic factors, they would not have destroyed the Empire unless they had made it possible for barbarians to invade the frontiers.

Finally, when we speak of the fall of Rome, we tacitly acquiesce in the judgment imposed by Gibbon. But even the fall of the Western Empire is an ambiguous historical event. The disappearance of the Empire can be interpreted in another way—as the transformation of this system into the states of medieval and then modern Europe. Our last selection, by Solomon Katz, carries us forward into these more recent times by showing that Roman civilization never really disappeared, even though the "Senate and People" of Rome no longer controlled their once vast domains in the West. Several of our modern languages, the Christian religion, and especially our law on both sides of the Atlantic, all descend from the Empire in a perfectly clear line of tradition. Some ancient empires, unlike that of Rome, not only passed away but exercise no important and lasting effect on mankind today. The Hittite, Egyptian, and perhaps even Athenian empires have left very little trace in today's world. But so long as we retain and strengthen the rule of law, which protects the otherwise vulnerable private citizen, we testify that the historical legacy of the Roman Empire is still active and beneficent.

To review the problem of the fall of Rome through a study of representative discussions is an unusually valuable undertaking for the student of history. This is no minor historical event about which source material is scanty or trivial. As we have seen, it was observed and recorded by contemporaries and near contemporaries; and in later times it has been the subject of many studies by major scholars with different points of view. By criticizing and evaluating these modern theories, the reader will learn to sharpen his own tools of historical analysis. And, since change and transformation of political systems are encountered in all periods of history, we may acquire permanently useful methods of thinking from a careful study of the fall of Rome.[2]

---

[2] By permission of the publishers, the selections that follow are, with a few exceptions, reprinted without the footnotes found in the original publications.

EDWARD GIBBON (1737–1794) issued the first
volume of *The History of the Decline and Fall
of the Roman Empire* in 1776 and the last three of the
six volumes in 1788. This work remains the
noblest literary masterwork in the field of history.
Gibbon regarded the fall of Rome as one of history's
great tragedies and accepted the canonical date, 476.
The selection printed here is Gibbon's conclusion
to volume III (1781). We may notice Gibbon's
belief, common among eighteenth-century thinkers,
that enlightened statesmanship could continue to
guide political events. He also believed that reason
and the spirit of progress were now strong enough
to guarantee European civilization against any threat
of destruction. Could an historian say this today?

Edward Gibbon

The Decline and Fall
of the Roman Empire

General Observations on the Fall
of the Roman Empire in the West

The Greeks, after their country had
been reduced into a province, imputed
the triumphs of Rome, not to the merit,
but to the FORTUNE, of the republic.
The inconstant goddess, who so blindly
distributes and resumes her favours, had
now consented (such was the language of
envious flattery) to resign her wings, to
descend from her globe, and to fix her
firm and immutable throne on the banks
of the Tiber. A wiser Greek, who has
composed, with a philosophic spirit, the
memorable history of his own times, deprived his countrymen of this vain and
delusive comfort by opening to their
view the deep foundations of the greatness of Rome.* The fidelity of the citizens to each other, and to the state, was
confirmed by the habits of education and
the prejudices of religion. Honour, as
well as virtue, was the principle of the
republic; the ambitious citizens laboured
to deserve the solemn glories of a triumph; and the ardour of the Roman
youth was kindled into active emulation,
as often as they beheld the domestic
images of their ancestors. The temperate
struggles of the patricians and plebeians
had finally established the firm and equal
balance of the constitution; which united
the freedom of popular assemblies with
the authority and wisdom of a senate
and the executive powers of a regal
magistrate. When the consul displayed
the standard of the republic, each citizen
bound himself, by the obligation of an
oath, to draw his sword in the cause of
his country, till he had discharged the
sacred duty by a military service of ten

* Polybius, especially in his Book 6—Ed.

7

years. This wise institution continually poured into the field the rising generations of freemen and soldiers; and their numbers were reinforced by the warlike and populous states of Italy, who, after a brave resistance, had yielded to the valour, and embraced the alliance, of the Romans. The sage historian, who excited the virtue of the younger Scipio and beheld the ruin of Carthage, has accurately described their military system; their levies, arms, exercises, subordination, marches, encampments; and the invincible legion, superior in active strength to the Macedonian phalanx of Philip and Alexander. From these institutions of peace and war, Polybius has deduced the spirit and success of a people incapable of fear and impatient of repose. The ambitious design of conquest, which might have been defeated by the seasonable conspiracy of mankind, was attempted and achieved; and the perpetual violation of justice was maintained by the political virtues of prudence and courage. The arms of the republic, sometimes vanquished in battle, always victorious in war, advanced with rapid steps to the Euphrates, the Danube, the Rhine, and the Ocean; and the images of gold, or silver, or brass, that might serve to represent the nations and their kings, were successively broken by the *iron* monarchy of Rome.

The rise of a city, which swelled into an empire, may deserve, as a singular prodigy, the reflection of a philosophic mind. But the decline of Rome was the natural and inevitable effect of immoderate greatness. Prosperity ripened the principle of decay; the causes of destruction multiplied with the extent of conquest; and, as soon as time or accident had removed the artificial supports, the stupendous fabric yielded to the pressure of its own weight. The story of its ruin is simple and obvious; and, instead of inquiring why the Roman empire was destroyed, we should rather be surprised that it had subsisted so long. The victorious legions, who, in distant wars, acquired the vices of strangers and mercenaries, first oppressed the freedom of the republic, and afterwards violated the majesty of the purple. The emperors, anxious for their personal safety and the public peace, were reduced to the base expedient of corrupting the discipline which rendered them alike formidable to their sovereign and to the enemy; the vigour of the military government was relaxed, and finally dissolved, by the partial institutions of Constantine; and the Roman world was overwhelmed by a deluge of Barbarians.

The decay of Rome has been frequently ascribed to the translation of the seat of empire;* but this history has already shewn that the powers of government were *divided* rather than *removed*. The throne of Constantinople was erected in the East; while the West was still possessed by a series of emperors who held their residence in Italy and claimed their equal inheritance of the legions and provinces. This dangerous novelty impaired the strength, and fomented the vices, of a double reign; the instruments of an oppressive and arbitrary system were multiplied; and a vain emulation of luxury, not of merit, was introduced and supported between the degenerate successors of Theodosius. Extreme distress, which unites the virtue of a free people, embitters the factions of a declining monarchy. The hostile favourites of Arcadius and Honorius betrayed the republic to its common enemies; and the Byzantine court beheld with indifference, perhaps with pleasure, the disgrace of Rome, the misfortunes

* From Rome to Constantinople—Ed.

of Italy, and the loss of the West. Under the succeeding reigns, the alliance of the two empires was restored; but the aid of the Oriental Romans was tardy, doubtful, and ineffectual; and the national schism of the Greeks and Latins was enlarged by the perpetual difference of language and manners, of interest, and even of religion. Yet the salutary event approved in some measure the judgment of Constantine. During a long period of decay, his impregnable city repelled the victorious armies of Barbarians, protected the wealth of Asia, and commanded, both in peace and war, the important straits which connect the Euxine and Mediterranean seas. The foundation of Constantinople more essentially contributed to the preservation of the East than to the ruin of the West.

As the happiness of a *future* life is the great object of religion, we may hear, without surprise or scandal, that the introduction, or at least the abuse, of Christianity had some influence on the decline and fall of the Roman empire. The clergy successfully preached the doctrines of patience and pusillanimity; the active virtues of society were discouraged; and the last remains of the military spirit were buried in the cloister; a large portion of public and private wealth was consecrated to the specious demands of charity and devotion; and the soldiers' pay was lavished on the useless multitudes of both sexes, who could only plead the merits of abstinence and chastity. Faith, zeal, curiosity, and the more earthly passions of malice and ambition kindled the flame of theological discord; the church, and even the state, were distracted by religious factions, whose conflicts were sometimes bloody, and always implacable; the attention of the emperors was diverted from camps to synods; the Roman world

was oppressed by a new species of tyranny; and the persecuted sects became the secret enemies of their country. Yet party-spirit, however pernicious or absurd, is a principle of union as well as of dissension. The bishops, from eighteen hundred pulpits, inculcated the duty of passive obedience to a lawful and orthodox sovereign; their frequent assemblies, and perpetual correspondence, maintained the communion of distant churches: and the benevolent temper of the gospel was strengthened, though confined, by the spiritual alliance of the Catholics. The sacred indolence of the monks was devoutly embraced by a servile and effeminate age; but, if superstition had not afforded a decent retreat, the same vices would have tempted the unworthy Romans to desert, from baser motives, the standard of the republic. Religious precepts are easily obeyed, which indulge and sanctify the natural inclinations of their votaries; but the pure and genuine influence of Christianity may be traced in its beneficial, though imperfect, effects on the Barbarian proselytes of the North. If the decline of the Roman empire was hastened by the conversion of Constantine, his victorious religion broke the violence of the fall, and mollified the ferocious temper of the conquerors.

This awful revolution may be usefully applied to the instruction of the present age. It is the duty of a patriot to prefer and promote the exclusive interest and glory of his native country; but a philosopher may be permitted to enlarge his views, and to consider Europe as one great republic, whose various inhabitants have attained almost the same level of politeness and cultivation. The balance of power will continue to fluctuate, and the prosperity of our own or the neighbouring kingdoms may be alternately exalted or depressed; but these partial events cannot essentially injure our general state of happiness, the system of arts, and laws, and manners, which so advantageously distinguish, above the rest of mankind, the Europeans and their colonies. The savage nations of the globe are the common enemies of civilized society; and we may inquire with anxious curiosity, whether Europe is still threatened with a repetition of those calamities which formerly oppressed the arms and institutions of Rome. Perhaps the same reflections will illustrate the fall of that mighty empire, and explain the probable causes of our actual security.

I. The Romans were ignorant of the extent of their danger, and the number of their enemies. Beyond the Rhine and Danube, the northern countries of Europe and Asia were filled with innumerable tribes of hunters and shepherds, poor, voracious, and turbulent; bold in arms, and impatient to ravish the fruits of industry. The Barbarian world was agitated by the rapid impulse of war; and the peace of Gaul or Italy was shaken by the distant revolutions of China. The Huns, who fled before a victorious enemy, directed their march towards the West; and the torrent was swelled by the gradual accession of captives and allies. The flying tribes who yielded to the Huns assumed in *their* turn the spirit of conquest; the endless column of Barbarians pressed on the Roman empire with accumulated weight; and, if the foremost were destroyed, the vacant space was instantly replenished by new assailants. Such formidable emigrations can no longer issue from the North; and the long repose, which has been imputed to the decrease of population, is the happy consequence of the progress of arts and

agriculture. Instead of some rude villages, thinly scattered among its woods and morasses, Germany now produces a list of two thousand three hundred walled towns; the Christian kingdoms of Denmark, Sweden, and Poland, have been successively established; and the Hanse merchants, with the Teutonic knights, have extended their colonies along the coast of the Baltic, as far as the Gulf of Finland. From the Gulf of Finland to the Eastern Ocean, Russia now assumes the form of a powerful and civilized empire. The plough, the loom, and the forge, are introduced on the banks of the Volga, the Oby, and the Lena; and the fiercest of the Tartar hordes have been taught to tremble and obey. The reign of independent Barbarism is now contracted to a narrow span; and the remnant of Calmucks or Uzbecks, whose forces may be almost numbered, cannot seriously excite the apprehensions of the great republic of Europe. Yet this apparent security should not tempt us to forget that new enemies, and unknown dangers, may *possibly* arise from some obscure people, scarcely visible in the map of the world. The Arabs or Saracens, who spread their conquests from India to Spain, had languished in poverty and contempt, till Mahomet breathed into those savage bodies the soul of enthusiasm.

II. The empire of Rome was firmly established by the singular and perfect coalition of its members. The subject nations, resigning the hope, and even the wish, of independence, embraced the character of Roman citizens; and the provinces of the West were reluctantly torn by the Barbarians from the bosom of their mother-country. But this union was purchased by the loss of national freedom and military spirit; and the servile provinces, destitute of life and motion, expected their safety from the mercenary troops and governors, who were directed by the orders of a distant court. The happiness of an hundred millions depended on the personal merit of one or two men, perhaps children, whose minds were corrupted by education, luxury, and despotic power. The deepest wounds were inflicted on the empire during the minorities of the sons and grandsons of Theodosius; and, after those incapable princes seemed to attain the age of manhood, they abandoned the church to the bishops, the state to the eunuchs, and the provinces to the Barbarians. Europe is now divided into twelve powerful, though unequal, kingdoms, three respectable commonwealths, and a variety of smaller, though independent, states; the chances of royal and ministerial talents are multiplied, at least with the number of its rulers; and a Julian, or Semiramis, may reign in the North, while Arcadius and Honorius again slumber on the thrones of the South. The abuses of tyranny are restrained by the mutual influence of fear and shame; republics have acquired order and stability; monarchies have imbibed the principles of freedom, or, at least, of moderation; and some sense of honour and justice is introduced into the most defective constitutions by the general manners of the times. In peace, the progress of knowledge and industry is accelerated by the emulation of so many active rivals: in war, the European forces are exercised by temperate and undecisive contests. . . .

III. Cold, poverty, and a life of danger and fatigue, fortify the strength and courage of Barbarians. In every age they have oppressed the polite and peaceful nations of China, India, and Persia, who neglected, and still neglect, to counterbalance these natural powers by the resources of military art. The warlike states of antiquity, Greece, Macedonia, and Rome, educated a race of soldiers; exercised their bodies, disciplined their courage, multiplied their forces by regular evolutions, and converted the iron which they possessed, into strong and serviceable weapons. But this superiority insensibly declined with their laws and manners; and the feeble policy of Constantine and his successors armed and instructed, for the ruin of the empire, the rude valour of the Barbarian mercenaries. The military art has been changed by the invention of gunpowder; which enables man to command the two most powerful agents of nature, air and fire. Mathematics, chymistry, mechanics, architecture, have been applied to the service of war; and the adverse parties oppose to each other the most elaborate modes of attack and of defence. Historians may indignantly observe that the preparations of a siege would found and maintain a flourishing colony; yet we cannot be displeased that the subversion of a city should be a work of cost and difficulty, or that an industrious people should be protected by those arts, which survive and supply the decay of military virtue. Cannon and fortifications now form an impregnable barrier against the Tartar horse; and Europe is secure from any future irruption of Barbarians; since, before they can conquer, they must cease to be barbarous. Their gradual advances in the science of war would always be accompanied, as we may learn from the example of Russia, with a proportionable improvement in the arts of peace and civil policy; and they themselves must deserve a place among the polished nations whom they subdue.

Should these speculations be found doubtful or fallacious, there still remains a more humble source of comfort and hope. The discoveries of ancient and modern navigators, and the domestic history, or tradition, of the most enlightened nations, represent the *human savage*, naked both in mind and body, and destitute of laws, of arts, of ideas, and almost of language. From this abject condition, perhaps the primitive and universal state of man, he has gradually arisen to command the animals, to fertilise the earth, to traverse the ocean, and to measure the heavens. His progress in the improvement and exercise of his mental and corporeal faculties has been irregular and various, infinitely slow in the beginning, and increasing by degrees with redoubled velocity; ages of laborious ascent have been followed by a moment of rapid downfall; and the several climates of the globe have felt the vicissitudes of light and darkness. Yet the experience of four thousand years should enlarge our hopes, and diminish our apprehensions; we cannot determine to what height the human species may aspire in their advances towards perfection; but it may safely be presumed that no people, unless the face of nature is changed, will relapse into their original barbarism. The improvements of society may be viewed under a threefold aspect. 1. The poet or philosopher illustrates his age and country by the efforts of a *single* mind; but these superior powers of reason or fancy are rare and spontaneous productions, and the genius of Homer, or Cicero, or Newton, would excite less admiration, if they could be created by the will of a prince or the lessons of a preceptor. 2. The benefits of law and policy, of trade and manufactures, of arts and sciences, are more solid and permanent; and *many* individuals may be qualified, by education and discipline, to promote,

in their respective stations, the interest of the community. But this general order is the effect of skill and labour; and the complex machinery may be decayed by time or injured by violence. 3. Fortunately for mankind, the more useful, or, at least, more necessary arts can be performed without superior talents or national subordination; without the powers of *one* or the union of *many*. Each village, each family, each individual, must always possess both ability and inclination to perpetuate the use of fire and of metals; the propagation and service of domestic animals; the methods of hunting and fishing; the rudiments of navigation; the imperfect cultivation of corn or other nutritive grain; and the simple practice of the mechanic trades. Private genius and public industry may be extirpated; but these hardy plants survive the tempest, and strike an everlasting root into the most unfavourable soil. The splendid days of Augustus and Trajan were eclipsed by a cloud of ignorance; and the Barbarians subverted the laws and palaces of Rome. But the scythe, the invention or emblem of Saturn, still continued annually to mow the harvests of Italy: and the human feasts of the Læstrygons* have never been renewed on the coast of Campania.

Since the first discovery of the arts, war, commerce, and religious zeal have diffused, among the savages of the Old and New World, those inestimable gifts: they have been successively propagated; they can never be lost. We may therefore acquiesce in the pleasing conclusion that every age of the world has increased, and still increases, the real wealth, the happiness, the knowledge, and perhaps the virtue, of the human race.

* Fabulous cannibals described in Homer's *Odyssey*—Ed.

Well-known for his outstanding single-volume
treatment of the *History of Greece*, J. B. BURY (1861–
1927) made his major field of research Byzantine
history. His reputation established with his
History of the Later Roman Empire in 1889, he became
Professor of Modern History at Cambridge
University from 1902 until his death. One of Bury's
theses, reflected in the following excerpts, was that
the Empire continued long after 476. In this respect
he challenged Gibbon, whose *Decline and Fall*
he edited. Bury also acted as an editor of the first
six volumes of the *Cambridge Ancient History*.
His interests led him to become one of the first
English-speaking historians to use Russian and other
Slavonic languages in his work.*

J. B. Bury

The Later Roman Empire

Modern Views on the Collapse of the Empire

The explanations of the calamities of
the Empire which have been hazarded
by modern writers are of a different
order from those which occurred to wit-
nesses of the events, but they are not
much more satisfying. The illustrious
historian whose name will always be associated with the "Decline" of the Roman
Empire invoked "the principle of decay,"
a principle which has itself to be explained. Depopulation, the Christian
religion, the fiscal system have all been
assigned as causes of the Empire's decline
in strength. If these or any of them were
responsible for its dismemberment by the
barbarians in the West, it may be asked
how it was that in the East, where the
same causes operated, the Empire survived much longer intact and united.

Consider depopulation. The depopulation of Italy was an important fact and
it had far-reaching consequences. But
it was a process which had probably
reached its limit in the time of Augustus.
There is no evidence that the Empire
was less populous in the fourth and fifth
centuries than in the first. The "sterility
of the human harvest" in Italy and
Greece affected the history of the Empire
from its very beginning, but does not
explain the collapse in the fifth century.
The truth is that there are two distinct

---

* From J. B. Bury, *History of the Later Roman Empire* (London. rev. ed., 1923), vol. I.
Reprinted by permission of Macmillan & Co. Ltd. and St. Martin's Press, Inc., New York.

questions which have been confused. It is one thing to seek the causes which changed the Roman State from what it was in the best days of the Republic to what it had become in the age of Theodosius the Great—a change which from certain points of view may be called a "decline." It is quite another thing to ask why the State which could resist its enemies on many frontiers in the days of Diocletian and Constantine and Julian suddenly gave way in the days of Honorius. "Depopulation" may partly supply the answer to the first question, but it is not an answer to the second. Nor can the events which transferred the greater part of western Europe to German masters be accounted for by the numbers of the peoples who invaded it. The notion of vast hosts of warriors, numbered by hundreds of thousands, pouring over the frontiers, is ... perfectly untrue. The total number of one of the large East German nations probably seldom exceeded 100,000, and its army of fighting men can rarely have been more than from 20,000 to 30,000. They were not a deluge, overwhelming and irresistible, and the Empire had a well-organised military establishment at the end of the fourth century, fully sufficient in capable hands to beat them back. As a matter of fact, since the defeat at Hadrianople which was due to the blunders of Valens, no very important battle was won by German over Imperial forces during the whole course of the invasions.

It has often been alleged that Christianity in its political effects was a disintegrating force and tended to weaken the power of Rome to resist her enemies. It is difficult to see that it had any such tendency, so long as the Church itself was united. Theological heresies were indeed to prove a disintegrating force in the East in the seventh century, when differences in doctrine which had alienated the Christians in Egypt and Syria from the government of Constantinople facilitated the conquests of the Saracens. But, after the defeat of Arianism, there was no such vital or deep-reaching division in the West, and the effect of Christianity was to unite, not to sever, to check, rather than to emphasise, national or sectional feeling. In the political calculations of Constantine it was probably this ideal of unity, as a counterpoise to the centrifugal tendencies which had been clearly revealed in the third century, that was the great recommendation of the religion which he raised to power. Nor is there the least reason to suppose that Christian teaching had the practical effect of making men less loyal to the Empire or less ready to defend it. The Christians were as pugnacious as the pagans. Some might read Augustine's *City of God* with edification, but probably very few interpreted its theory with such strict practical logic as to be indifferent to the safety of the Empire. Hardly the author himself, though this has been disputed.

It was not long after Alaric's capture of Rome that Volusian, a pagan senator of a distinguished family, whose mother was a Christian and a friend of Augustine, proposed the question whether the teaching of Christianity is not fatal to the welfare of a State, because a Christian smitten on one cheek would if he followed the precepts of the Gospel turn the other to the smiter. We have the letter in which Augustine answers the question and skilfully explains the text so as to render it consistent with common sense. And to show that warfare is not forbidden another text is quoted in which soldiers who ask "What shall we do?" are bidden to "Do violence to no man, neither accuse any falsely, and be content with your wages." They are not told not to serve or fight. The bishop goes on to suggest that those who wage a just war are really acting *misericorditer,* in a spirit of mercy and kindness to their enemies, as it is to the true interests of their enemies that their vices should be corrected. Augustine's *misericorditer* laid down unintentionally a dangerous and hypocritical doctrine for the justification of war, the same principle which was used for justifying the Inquisition. But his definite statement that the Christian discipline does not condemn all wars was equivalent to saying that Christians were bound as much as pagans to defend Rome against the barbarians. And this was the general view. All the leading Churchmen of the fifth century were devoted to the Imperial idea, and when they worked for peace or compromise, as they often did, it was always when the cause of the barbarians was in the ascendant and resistance seemed hopeless.

The truth is that the success of the barbarians in penetrating and founding states in the western provinces cannot be explained by any general considerations. It is accounted for by the actual events and would be clearer if the story were known more fully. The gradual collapse of the Roman power in this section of the Empire was the consequence of *a series of contingent events.* No general causes can be assigned that made it inevitable.

The first contingency was the irruption of the Huns into Europe, an event resulting from causes which were quite independent of the weakness or strength of the Roman Empire. It drove the Visigoths into the Illyrian provinces, and the difficult situation was unhappily mismanaged. One Emperor was defeated and lost his life;* it was his own fault. That disaster, which need not have occurred, was a second contingency. His successor allowed a whole federate nation to settle on provincial soil; he took the line of least resistance and established an unfortunate precedent.† He did not foresee consequences which, if he had lived ten or twenty years longer, might not have ensued. His death was a third contingency. But the situation need have given no reason for grave alarm if the succession had passed to an Emperor like himself, or Valentinian I., or even Gratian. Such a man was not procreated by Theodosius and the government of the West was inherited by a feeble-minded boy.** That was a fourth event, dependent on causes which had nothing to do with the condition of the Empire.

In themselves these events need not have led to disaster. If the guardian of Honorius and director of his government had been a man of Roman birth and tradition,†† who commanded the public confidence, a man such as Honorius himself was afterwards to find in Constantius and his successor in Aetius, all might have been tolerably well. But there was a point of weakness in the Imperial system, the practice of elevating Germans to the highest posts of command in the army. It had grown up under Valentinian I., Gratian, and Theodosius; it had led to the rebellion of Maximus, and had cost Valentinian II. his life. The German in whom Theodosius reposed his confidence and who assumed the control of affairs on his death

* Valens, defeated in 378 at Adrianople—Ed.
† Theodosius I allowed the Goths to settle south of the Danube in 382—Ed.
** Honorius—Ed.
†† Stilicho was a Romanized German—Ed.

probably believed that he was serving Rome faithfully, but it was a singular misfortune that at a critical moment when the Empire had to be defended not only against Germans without but against a German nation which had penetrated inside, the responsibility should have devolved upon a German. Stilicho did not intend to be a traitor, but his policy was as calamitous as if he had planned deliberate treachery. For it meant civil war. The dissatisfaction of the Romans in the West was expressed in the rebellion of Constantine, the successor of Maximus, and if Stilicho had had his way the soldiers of Honorius and of Arcadius would have been killing one another for the possession of Illyricum. When he died the mischief was done; Goths had Italy at their mercy, Gaul and Spain were overrun by other peoples. His Roman successors could not undo the results of events which need never have happened.

The supremacy of a Stilicho was due to the fact that the defence of the Empire had come to depend on the enrolment of barbarians, in large numbers, in the army, and that it was necessary to render the service attractive to them by the prospect of power and wealth. This was, of course, a consequence of the decline in military spirit, and of depopulation, in the old civilised Mediterranean countries. The Germans in high command had been useful, but the dangers involved in the policy had been shown in the cases of Merobaudes and Arbogastes. Yet this policy need not have led to the dismemberment of the Empire, and but for that series of chances its western provinces would not have been converted, as and when they were, into German kingdoms. It may be said that a German penetration of western Europe must ultimately have come about. But even if that were certain, it might have happened in another way, at a later time, more gradually, and with less violence. The point of the present contention is that Rome's loss of her provinces in the fifth century was not an "inevitable effect of any of those features which have been rightly or wrongly described as causes or consequences of her general 'decline.' " The central fact that Rome could not dispense with the help of barbarians for her wars (*gentium barbararum auxilio indigemus*) may be held to be the cause of her calamities, but it was a weakness which might have continued to be far short of fatal but for the sequence of contingencies pointed out above.

The Rise of Odovacar and His Rule in Italy (A.D. 473—489)

After the death of Olybrius, Leo was sole Roman Emperor for more than four months, and the Burgundian Gundobad, who had succeeded his uncle Ricimer as Master of Soldiers, directed the conduct of affairs in Italy. On March 5, A.D. 473, Glycerius, Count of the Domestics, was proclaimed Emperor at Ravenna "by the advice of Gundobad," just as Severus had been proclaimed in the same city by the advice of Ricimer. Of this Augustus, whose reign was to be brief, one important public act is recorded. Italy was threatened by an invasion of Ostrogoths who, under the leadership of Widemir, began to move from Pannonia, but the diplomacy of Glycerius averted the storm, so that it fell on Gaul.

The election of Glycerius was not approved at Constantinople, and Leo selected another as the successor of Anthemius. His choice was Julius Nepos, husband of the niece of the Empress, and military governor of Dalmatia, where he had succeeded his uncle, count Marcellinus. We do not hear that any resistance was offered to Nepos, who arrived in Italy, probably escorted by eastern troops; and it was not long before Gundobad, whether perforce or voluntarily, retired to Burgundy where, in the following year, he succeeded his father as one of the Burgundian kings. Glycerius was deposed, and at Portus, the town at the mouth of the Tiber, he was ordained bishop of Salona. Nepos was proclaimed Emperor and ruled at Rome (June 24, A.D. 474). Once more two Augusti reigned in unison.

To the vacant post of Master of Soldiers, which carried with it almost as a matter of course the title of Patrician, Orestes was appointed. This was that Orestes who had been the secretary of Attila, and he had married the daughter of a certain count Romulus. Possessing the confidence of the German troops he determined to raise his son to the Imperial throne.

We are told that Nepos, driven from Rome, went to Ravenna and, fearing the coming of Orestes, crossed over to Salona. This was on August 28, A.D. 475. The same year that saw the flight of Zeno from Constantinople saw the flight of Nepos from Ravenna. At Salona he lived for five years, and his Imperial authority was still recognised in the East and in Gaul. But in Italy the Caesar Julius was succeeded by the Caesar Augustulus, for so the young Romulus was mockingly nicknamed, whom his father Orestes invested with the Imperial insignia on October 31. These names, Julius, Augustulus, Romulus, in the pages of the chroniclers, meet us like ghosts re-arisen from past days of Roman history.

It is important to remember that the position of Romulus was not constitutional inasmuch as he had not been recognized by the Emperor at Constantinople, in whose eyes Nepos was still the Augustus of the West. For twelve months Orestes ruled Italy in the name of his son. His fall was brought about by a mutiny of the troops. The army, which the Master of Soldiers commanded, seems to have consisted under Ricimer and his successors almost exclusively of East Germans, chiefly Heruls, also Rugians and Scirians. According to the usual custom, they were quartered on the Italians. But they were weary of this life. They desired to have roof-trees and lands of their own, and they petitioned Orestes to reward them for their services, by granting them lands and settling them permanently in Italy on the same principle on which various German peoples had been settled in other provinces. They did not demand the exceptionally large concession of two-thirds of the soil which had been granted by Honorius to the Visigoths; they asked for the normal grant of one-third which had been assigned, for instance, to the Burgundians. But such a settlement in Italy was a very different thing from settlement in Gaul or Spain, and Orestes, notwithstanding his long association with Germans and Huns, was sufficiently Roman to be determined to keep the soil of Italy inviolate. He rejected the demand. The discontented soldiers found a leader in the Scirian Odovacar, one of the chief officers of Orestes. Ticinum to which Orestes retired was easily taken, and the Patrician was slain at Placentia (August 28, A.D. 476). "Entering Ravenna, Odovacar deposed Augustulus but granted him his life, pitying his infancy and because he was comely, and he gave him an income of six thousand solidi and sent him to live in Campania with his relatives."

The soldiers had proclaimed Odovacar king. But it was not as king over a mixed host of various German nationalities that Odovacar thought he could maintain his position in Italy. The movement which had raised him had no national significance, and if he retained the royal title of an East German potentate, it was as a successor of Ricimer, Gundobad, and Orestes that he hoped to govern the Italians. In other words, he had no idea of detaching Italy from the Empire, as Africa and much of Gaul and Spain had come to be detached. The legal position was to continue as before. But the system of Ricimer was to be abandoned. There were to be no more puppet Emperors in the West; Italy was to be under the sovranty of the Emperor at Constantinople, and its actual government was to be in the hands of Odovacar, who as Master of Soldiers was to be a minister of the Emperor, while he happened at the same time to be king of the East Germans who formed the army.

With this purpose in view Odovacar made the deposition of Romulus take the form of an abdication, and induced the Roman Senate to endorse formally the permanent institution of a state of things which had repeatedly existed in the days of Ricimer. A deputation of senators, in the name of Romulus, was sent to the Augustus at Constantinople to announce the new order of things. Zeno had already recovered the throne, from which Basiliscus had driven him, when the ambassadors arrived and informed him that they no longer needed a separate Emperor but that his sole supremacy would be sufficient; that they had selected Odovacar as a man capable of protecting Italy, being both a tried soldier and endowed with political intelligence. They asked Zeno to confer upon him the rank of Patrician and entrust him with the administration of Italy. They bore with them the Imperial insignia which Romulus had worn (A.D. 477).

At the same time messengers arrived from Nepos to congratulate Zeno on his restoration, to ask for his sympathy with one who had suffered the same misfortune as he, and to crave his aid in men and money to recover the throne. But for the existence of Nepos, the situation would have been simple. Zeno could not ignore his legal right, but was not prepared to support it with an army. He told the representatives of the Senate that of the two Emperors they had received from the East, they had slain Anthemius and banished Nepos; let them now take Nepos back. But he granted the other request. He sent to Odovacar a diploma conferring the Patriciate, and wrote to him, praising the respect for Rome and the observance of order which had marked his conduct, and bidding him crown his goodness by acknowledging the exiled Emperor. The fact that Verina was the aunt of the wife of Nepos was a consideration which helped to hinder Zeno from disowning him. Odovacar did not acknowledge the claim of Nepos, and Zeno cannot have expected that he would.

The events of A.D. 476 have been habitually designated as the "Fall of the Western Empire." The phrase is inaccurate and unfortunate, and sets the changes which befell in a false light. No Empire fell in A.D. 476; there was no

"Western Empire" to fall. There was only one Roman Empire, which sometimes was governed by two or more Augusti. If it is replied that the expression is merely a convenient one to signify what contemporary writers sometimes called the Hesperian realm (*Hesperium regnum*), the provinces which had been, since the death of Theodosius I., generally under the separate government of an Emperor residing in Italy, and that all that is meant is the termination of this line of western Emperors, it may be pointed out that A.D. 480 is in that case the significant date. For Julius Nepos, who died in that year, was the last legitimate Emperor in the West; Romulus Augustulus was only a usurper. The important point to seize is that, from the constitutional point of view, Odovacar was the successor of Ricimer, and that the situation created by the events of A.D. 476 was in this respect similar to the situation in the intervals between the reigns of the Emperors set up by Ricimer. If, on the death of Honorius, there had been no Valentinian to succeed him, and if Theodosius II. had exercised the sovranty over the western provinces, and if no second Augustus had been created again before the western provinces had passed under the sway of Teutonic rulers, no one would have spoken of the "Fall of the Western Empire." Yet this hypothetical case would be formally the same as the actual event of A.D. 476 or rather of A.D. 480. The West came finally, as it had more than once come temporarily, under the sole sovranty of the Emperor reigning at East Rome.

The Italian revolution of A.D. 476 was, however, a most memorable event, though it has been wrongly described. It stands out prominently as an im-

portant stage in the process of the dismemberment of the Empire. It belongs to the same catalogue of chronological dates which includes A.D. 418, when Honorius settled the Goths in Aquitaine, and A.D. 435, when Valentinian ceded African lands to the Vandals. In A.D. 476 the same principle of disintegration was first applied to Italy. The settlement of Odovacar's East Germans, with Zeno's acquiescence, began the process by which Italian soil was to pass into the hands of Ostrogoths and Lombards, Franks and Normans. And Odovacar's title of king emphasised the significance of the change.

It is highly important to observe that Odovacar established his political power with the co-operation of the Roman Senate, and this body seems to have given him their loyal support throughout his reign, so far as our meagre sources permit us to draw inferences. At this time the senators who counted politically belonged to a few old and distinguished clans, possessing large estates and great wealth, particularly the Decii and the Anicii. The leading men of these families received high honours and posts under Odovacar. Basilius, Decius, Venantius, and Manlius Boethius held the consulship and were either Prefects of Rome or Praetorian Prefects; Symmachus and Sividius were consuls and Prefects of Rome; another senator of old family, Cassiodorus, was appointed a minister of finance. The evidence indicates that while it was Odovacar's policy to appoint only men of Roman families to the Prefecture of the City, he allowed the Prefect to hold office only for a year, so that no man might win a dangerous political importance.

Yet the Roman nobility were now compelled to contribute more largely to the maintenance of the military forces which defended Italy. The greater part of the land belonged to them, and by the new settlement one-third of their estates was taken from the proprietors, and Odovacar's barbarian soldiers and their families were settled on them. It is not probable that the number of these soldiers exceeded 20,000 at the most, and it has been reasonably doubted whether this measure was actually carried out throughout the length and breadth of the peninsula. We may suspect that the needs of the army were satisfied without a drastic application of the principle of partition. If the illustrious landowners had been mulcted on a large scale, it is hardly credible that they would have co-operated with the king as loyally as they seem to have done.

Soon after the government of Italy had passed into his hands, Odovacar's diplomacy achieved a solid success by inducing Gaiseric, who died in January, A.D. 477, to cede to him the island of Sicily. He undertook indeed to pay for it a yearly tribute, and the Vandal king reserved a foothold in the island, doubtless the western fortress of Lilybaeum. The death of Julius Nepos has been mentioned. He was murdered by two of his retainers in his country house near Salona in May, A.D. 480. Odovacar assumed the duty of pursuing and executing the assassins, and at the same time established his own rule in Dalmatia. The claims of Nepos, so long as he lived, had embarrassed the relations between Zeno and Odovacar; Zeno's acquiescence in Odovacar's position and the wishes of the Senate had been ambiguous and reserved. The death of Nepos relieved the situation, and there was no longer any difficulty at Constantinople about acknowledging the western consuls whom Odovacar chose. But the relations between the Emperor and his Master of Soldiers in Italy were always strained, and in A.D. 486 there was an open breach. Though Odovacar did not help the rebel Illus in his revolt, there were negotiations, and Zeno may have been suspicious and alarmed. Odovacar prepared an expedition into the Illyrian provinces, then pressed hard by the Ostrogoths, and Zeno averted it by instigating the Rugians to invade Italy. Odovacar anticipated their attack by marching through Noricum and surprising them in the winter season (end of A.D. 487) in their territory beyond the Danube. Their king Feletheus and his queen were taken to Italy and beheaded, and with the death of his son, against whom a second expedition was sent, the Rugian power was destroyed.

Of the internal government we know little. The Church was unaffected by his rule; as an Arian he held aloof from ecclesiastical affairs. As to the working of the Roman administration under a German ruler, acting as an independent viceroy, and the limitations imposed on his power, we have abundant evidence regarding Odovacar's successor, Theoderic. . . .

The population of the Empire was threatened from the second century onward by recurrent plagues and wars. Beyond question, such conditions must have made it more difficult to maintain the economic and military stability of the Empire. But the precise degree to which a crisis in population contributed to the fall of Rome is warmly debated. The excerpt below on the decline of population within the Western Empire is by ARTHUR E. R. BOAK (1888–1962), a leading authority on the later Empire and for many years professor of history at the University of Michigan. He stresses particularly the plague of A.D. 166–180 and its continuing effects over some decades. Note that he carefully entitled his book a study of the decline of the Empire in the West.*

Arthur E. R. Boak

Manpower Shortage and
the Fall of Rome

...I shall try to sum up the conclusions at which I arrived in the foregoing chapters and also to correlate manpower shortage with the other major factors that contributed to the collapse of the West Roman Empire in the fifth century. Let me make it clear at this point that I do not believe there was any single major cause of this collapse, but rather a combination of conditions, forces, and trends which interacted upon one another so that at times it is almost impossible to tell which was cause and which was effect. Nor do I believe it possible to indicate with any degree of exactness the point at which recessions began. Furthermore, I do not believe there was uniformity of conditions through the Western Empire as a whole, and I am quite prepared to admit that the process of decay may for a time have been arrested and, within limited areas, even temporarily reversed.

It is my conviction that I have been able to present convincing reasons, partly on the basis of contemporary evidence and partly on the strength of deductions drawn from the demographic history of other peoples, for believing that a shortage in manpower had developed within the Roman Empire as early as the last quarter of the second century. In my opinion this shortage of manpower is to be associated with, and was caused by, an actual retrogression of certain elements of the population, in particular the inhabitants of the rural areas. In this I see the explanation of such a phenomenon as the inability of the Emperor Marcus Aurelius to find the needed recruits for his army among the Romans and provincials and his resort to the importation of barbarians to make up the deficit. By the beginning of the third century manpower shortage was felt to be affecting the population of the towns also. Here, as an important factor may be seen the legacy of the great plague of the years 166 to 180. At any rate, Septimius Severus and others of his dynasty admitted the situation and sought to combat by legislative means some of its consequences. Their attempts to encourage agriculture and increase the rural population, their closer supervision of the occupational groups whose services appeared essential to the conduct of public business, and their impressment of the town councils as tax collecting agencies reflect both a shortage in production and a scarcity of manpower. . . .

It would, of course, be utterly impossible to calculate the total population loss between the death of Marcus Aurelius in 180 and that of Severus Alexander in 235. It would be just as much out of the question to try to estimate the decline in the birth rate. There were almost certainly areas where such symptoms had not yet become apparent, for example, in sections of North Africa, where the municipalities continued to expand until later in the third century. But these favorable conditions were due to special circumstances and cannot be made the basis for generalizations about Italy and the western provinces as a whole.

It has been seen how the disorders of the troubled period 235 to 284 were bound to have an extremely unfavorable effect upon the population, both rural and urban. Not only must the actual loss of life have been extremely heavy and the average longevity correspondingly reduced, but the rate of decline must have been greatly accelerated. To judge from later parallels, the population of the Roman world can hardly have recovered from the delayed effects of the epidemic of the time of Marcus Aurelius before it was struck by the equally severe and even longer pestilence of the middle third century. Also, the added losses due to war, starvation, and forcible deportation must be taken into account. Once the birth rate of a people starts to decline, it continues to do so in a geometrical and not merely an arithmetical ratio. The conclusion must therefore be reached that if even a slight decline were evident by 235, as a result of total population loss, the rate would be very noticeable by 284. Furthermore, it would keep on becoming increasingly rapid unless or until a countertrend were established.

On the analogy of the experience of other countries, it would take a very long time even under favorable conditions for this countertrend to become effective. It is only too well known that such favorable conditions never came into being during the fourth and fifth centuries. And the evidence I have presented from the period 284–476 indicates that, in spite of the restoration of a large measure of internal peace, and notwithstanding the voluntary and involuntary immigration of barbarian peoples, the population trend was steadily downward until the end of the West Roman Empire. Herein lies the explanation of the continued decline in the population of western Europe until about 900, a phenomenon noted by students of medieval demography.

The inevitable accompaniment of the population decline was naturally a corresponding decrease in the manpower available for agriculture, industry, and the public services, a condition which became more and more acute from the late third to the fifth century. At the same time there was a corresponding decrease in agricultural and industrial production. It would be rash to say that this was due altogether to shortage of available labor since the economic policies of the Late Empire unquestionably played a considerable role in preventing a revival of prosperity. The decline in individual capital wealth was also a factor of importance. In general, both in agriculture and in industry, there was a very definite correlation between the number of workers available and the quantity of production. Insufficiency of agricultural production in its turn reacted upon the ability of the population to maintain itself. Taken together, all of these factors produced an overall condition of impoverishment which offers the fundamental explanation of the social and economic policy of the government of the Late Empire.

Undoubtedly, the ultimate objective of Diocletian and his successors was the preservation of the Empire. And it is equally beyond question that, with the exception of some weaklings in the West during the fifth century, the rulers of the Late Empire devoted themselves conscientiously and unsparingly to this task. It seems equally clear that for them the cardinal problems were the maintenance of internal order and the defense of the frontiers. Each of these problems required the presence of a strong, loyal, and efficient army. Since the peculiar geographical situation of the Roman Empire, strung out as it was around the shores of the Mediterranean Sea, gave it frontiers whose length was out of proportion to its superficial area, and since the internal lines of communication were correspondingly extended as well as interrupted by the Mediterranean and its tributary waters, the size of the standing army had to be considerably larger than would have been required in a more compact state. Furthermore, the frontiers were under continuous attack or threat of attack from Persians and barbarians, so that, far from reducing the military establishment, Diocletian felt that he must actually increase it. The emperors of the fourth century tried to maintain the army at the level set by him, or even to strengthen somewhat its effectives. There could be no question of their reviving the citizen militia armies of the days of the Republic. They had to accept the professional, long-service army developed under the Early Empire, although they might and did modify its internal organization.

As has been seen, in trying to enlarge and maintain such an army the emperors were faced with a shortage of suitable recruits, caused in large measure by the decline of the rural population. Hence they found themselves on the horns of a dilemma. Either they could conscript Roman civilians for military service and so decrease still further production and the state revenues, or they could adopt and employ on a larger scale the policy initiated by Marcus Aurelius, followed by other emperors, and resorted to much more widely by Probus, namely, to make up the deficit with barbarians. It would be naïve to think that the imperial government was blind to the dangers of such a policy. That they adopted it, is a clear indication of the acute problem of available manpower within the empire. It led, inevitably, to the gradual barbarization of the army, that is, to the predominance of the barbarian element both in the ranks and in the officer corps, even including the commanding generals. It led also to the wholesale settlement of barbarian colonies within the western provinces as feeders for the army. These groups were not assimilated into the Roman citizen body. A vigorous and expanding population could have absorbed them, but not the enfeebled and discouraged one of the Late Empire. Yet in spite of these settlements, shortage of manpower for the army continued and this, coupled with decreasing revenues, led the state to resort to the subsidization of actually autonomous, although nominally dependent, barbarian tribes as federate allies under the obligation to defend the frontiers. The inability of the Roman government to prevent the settlement of these allies as well as other invaders within the Empire, coupled with the passing of the command of the army of the West into the hands of barbarian king makers was the immediate cause of the disintegration of the Western Empire....

It has been held by some historians that it was not scarcity of recruits but lack of military spirit among the Romans that caused the emperors to depend to such a great extent upon barbarians. No doubt, under the system of recruitment which was practiced there was a tendency for the landholder to supply recruits of inferior physique who lacked the necessary military qualities. No doubt also,

there was a great deal of self-mutilation to avoid military service, and desertions were only too frequent. The reason why such a poor type of recruit was furnished by the Roman element is to be found in the lack of suitable men who could be spared from essential production, as well as in the indifference of the *coloni*[*] and other hereditary working groups toward the fate of a government which seemed to them more brutal in its exactions than did the barbarians. The Gauls, however, made excellent soldiers and so did the Illyrians, only there were not enough of them. Vegetius, in discussing the deficiency of suitable recruits, gives priority to decline of population over aversion to military life caused by urbanization.

Not only did the emperors require a large standing army to support their authority within the Empire and to defend it against attack from without, but they also had to maintain a system of civil government adequate for the administration of justice and, above all, for the collection of the taxes requisite for defraying the military and civil expenditures of the state. Here, again, they were the heirs of a long tradition which had resulted in the growth of a highly centralized bureaucracy. It would have been futile to think of replacing this with some decentralized system that might have been less expensive but, from the point of view of the emperors, less efficient and less subject to supervision and control. As it was, the attempt to enforce the economic and social reforms and to extract as large a revenue as possible from the civilian population led to increased departmentalization of the bureaucracy and also to an increase in the number of civil service employees. This coincided

[*] Tenant farmers—Ed.

with the replacement of imperial slaves and freedmen in the office staffs by salaried persons of free birth, a policy which had begun under the Early Empire and had been hastened by the decrease in the number of slaves available. As I have pointed out, the extent to which this produced a drain upon the civilian population cannot be estimated, but it did, undoubtedly, add to the number of nonproducers and correspondingly increased the cost of government. This in turn made the burden of the taxpayers still heavier and, under the declining economic conditions, led to further impoverishment. . . .

At this point, it might be worth while to consider briefly the view that the decrease in agricultural production was due to a condition of soil exhaustion which affected the Empire as a whole. I am in agreement with those who reject this theory. Beyond all question Greece, the Italian peninsula, and Sicily had suffered greatly from soil erosion and consequent soil impoverishment, which was an important factor in the decline of agriculture and of the rural population in these areas. But no such condition has been demonstrated for the Po Valley, the Rhine and Danubian lands, Gaul, Britain, and North Africa, or even for Spain, although it is possible that it had begun to affect parts of that peninsula. In the light of present knowledge of soil conditions in the Late Empire, the shortage of agricultural products must be attributed largely to shortage of rural labor and a failure to develop improved methods of cultivation and improved farm machinery which might have compensated for the decrease in manpower. . . .

Faced by this shortage of contractors and workers, the government resorted to conscription. By developing to the utmost the principle of public obligations incumbent on both persons and property they bound to the public service the capital and the persons deemed essential in the collecting of levies of all kinds and the proper handling of the various sorts of government supplies. Thus, the municipal councilors, the corporations of shipowners and transport workers, as well as the similar corporations of merchants and others engaged in processing or selling grain, wine, oil, and various sorts of meat for Rome (and later for Constantinople), found themselves reduced to the status of involuntary government employees. As members of these guilds or corporations they were compelled to serve the state either without, or at best with inadequate, compensation.

The same basic factor, the shortage of manpower for public service, brought about the impressment of the members of the municipal corporations throughout the Empire and of their capital into public service. The immediate reasons might vary from one type of corporation to another, but in every instance the underlying cause was an actual or a feared shortage of personnel for services which the imperial government deemed necessary for the proper maintenance of municipal life or for the proper performance of the part which the municipalities had to play in the whole system of local, provincial, and imperial administration. This obligation was extended even to the actors' guilds, whose members were bound just as strictly as were the carpenters, masons, and rug makers, who acted as the municipal fire brigades. The only distinction between the condition of these local guilds and that of those who served the needs of urban Rome was that their services were not so continuously in demand. Most of their *munera*, however, had to be performed without compensation. In addition, all persons engaged in trade and industry were subjected to an onerous tax collected in gold and silver money.

Another result of the shortage and uncertainties of production was the taking over by the state of the manufacturing of farms and armor and, to a larger extent, clothing for the army. This additional encroachment upon the field of private enterprise may have been somewhat motivated by a desire to maintain a government monopoly of weapons of warfare as a means of controlling brigandage and insurrection. But coming as it did upon the heels of the economic collapse in the third century, it finds its chief explanation in the inability of private manufacturers to supply government needs in this area of production. On the other hand, the state monopoly of the production of certain types of silk goods and of purple dyes was not so much the result of any shortage of production as of the desire to reserve for members of the imperial court and high government officials the use of silk garments and also of the purple dye which had come to be associated with autocracy. This was all in accordance with the policy of emphasizing the sacredness of the imperial household and the great gulf that separated the emperor from the rest of the population. Since the supply of silk in the Mediterranean area before the importation of the silkworm from China in the middle of the sixth century was very limited, the monopoly of the production of silk goods was easy to establish and maintain. Like the monopoly of the manufacture of red dyes from certain species of shellfish

which seem to have become scarce, that of silk manufacture had little effect upon the economy of the Empire in the West. As has been seen, however, in operating these enterprises as well as the government arsenals and clothing establishments, the state encountered difficulties arising from a shortage of labor. In its desperate attempt to maintain production it felt compelled to resort to the imposing of a permanent hereditary obligation upon its employees.

Having traced the part of manpower shortage in determining the military and economic policy of the Late Roman Empire, I shall now consider the effects of this policy upon the population situation. Did it create conditions under which population, and with it production, could increase and prosperity be restored? The answer is emphatically in the negative. The restoration of more peaceful internal conditions by the early fourth century did unquestionably lead to a temporary improvement in agriculture in some areas and to the rise of some new urban centers. And this improvement would naturally operate as a brake upon the rate of population decrease. But, unfortunately, it was neither general nor sustained. The crushing load of taxation and obligatory government services proved too great for the producing classes to support. They did not have the wherewithal to raise and support families large enough to maintain, much less increase, their numbers from one generation to the next. Their lives were so burdensome that each of the obligatory occupation groups sought to escape from its status. The army, the civil service, and the clergy seemed havens of refuge for many. Farm workers tried to enter one of the town corporations or deserted their fields to swell the numbers of brigands or to join troups of invading barbarians. Town councilors even sought to hide themselves as hereditary tenants on the estates of the great landholders. People of various classes took to the forests or the desert to avoid the eyes of government officials. The result was a still further decrease in the manpower available for private or public production. Under such circumstances the government reacted as might have been expected. It tried to tighten the system of controls by which it regulated the lives of the vast majority of the population. Law after law reiterated the life-long obligation of the individual to his particular class or corporation and its activities, the perpetual lien of the state, municipality, or college upon his property for financing the performance of its functions, the hereditability of his status by his heirs, the ban upon attempts to alter one's inherited condition, and the prohibition to change one's place of residence. But all to no purpose. Conditions grew steadily worse. By the early fifth century the area of untilled land had reached astonishing proportions, and many of the cities had become ghost towns.

But someone may raise the question, how is such a state of affairs compatible with the building activities of the emperors of the time, with the multitude of churches that arose in the fourth and fifth centuries in Italy and the western provinces, or with the opulence of the homes of the upper classes and the apparently. easy circumstances in which they lived? How can it be reconciled with the maintenance of the free distribution of food for the city proletariat of Rome at the expense of the govern-

ment? The explanation is not difficult. In so far as the emperors were concerned, they were caught in the toils of tradition and felt that as far as possible they must live up to the standards set by their predecessors. A display of public munificence had to be maintained if an emperor were not to lose prestige in the eyes of his subjects. And loss of prestige might foster discontent and lead to the support of a rival. It probably never even occurred to one of the late emperors to abandon the distribution of free bread, oil, and wine to the Roman mob, however much that might have reduced government expenses and however many persons and however much private capital it might have released for profitable enterprises. No better proof is required of the influence of tradition in this respect than Constantine's granting of similar donations to the residents of his new capital, Constantinople. But, as a matter of fact, after the age of Diocletian and Constantine I, few great buildings were erected in the western part of the Empire, and even for the adornment of Constantine's own arch in Rome an earlier monument had to be despoiled. A large number of the churches of the time were remodeled pagan temples or were built from the ruins of public buildings no longer requisite for the decreasing population of Rome and other cities, nor did they compare in size or elegance with the great structures of earlier days. The wealthy aristocracy of the Late Empire was composed of inner circles of the senatorial order. They were the great landholders who furnished the higher officials of the bureaucracy and, to some extent, of the army. Their estates grew as the smaller proprietors were sold out by the government or handed over their properties to their more influential neighbors and became their serfs rather than face the imperial tax collectors. They, too, acquired abandoned lands which the government offered to any who could afford to till them, and who but the very wealthy could do so? The majority of them no longer lived in the cities but in large country villas, at times fortified, surrounded by their dependent serfs. There, relying upon their influence in the administration and even at times resorting to armed force, they could mitigate or defy the demands of government agents. These few grew relatively richer, as the middle classes were reduced to beggary and almost disappeared, and the poorer sank to even lower levels of wretchedness.

It might possibly be asked, Why did not the extensive settlement of Germanic people within the Empire reverse the downward population trend in the rural areas? Possibly it did in some districts and during brief periods, for the Romans in earlier times considered that the families of these barbarians were larger than theirs. In many places the new settlers were numerous enough to have the memory of their presence perpetuated in the names of rural communities. But there is no proof of any permanent beneficial effects, and even after the settlement of the larger tribes of barbarian conquerors, the downward trend continued. For this the following observations may offer at least a partial explanation. The Germans, like the other peoples of ancient times, had a high rate of infant mortality and a low average longevity, both of which kept down the rate of population increase. Furthermore, the lot of those who were settled as *coloni* on the properties of rural proprietors was little removed from slavery. Like the rest of the peasants attached to the soil, they came to feel the double pressure of the demands of their landlords and of the state, and their share of their crops was reduced to the bare subsistence level. This gave no encouragement to the raising of any large families, but it did encourage desertion of the lands to which they were in bondage. A life of brigandage or the opportunity of joining a band of barbarian marauders would seem infinitely preferable to the thankless toil to which they had been condemned. On the other hand, those who were settled in groups on state land with the obligation to furnish recruits to the Roman army found their young men taken in large numbers into service. Although these were permitted to marry, their life was not conducive to the raising of a numerous progeny and their average longevity doubtless fell well below that of those not engaged in military service. At any rate, the ever-increasing shortage of recruits indicates that they were not very prolific since, as will be remembered, the sons of soldiers and veterans came to be obligated to follow the paternal profession. In this connection it may be worth while to repeat that for some centuries after the settlement of the larger barbarian tribes—Visigoths, Burgundians, Franks, and so forth—within the formers limits of the western Empire, no rise in population appears to have taken place.

MOSES I. FINLEY (1912–   ) is an American scholar
now teaching at Jesus College, Cambridge. His
major field of research has been economic history.
In his critique of Boak's demographic theory, he
maintains that manpower shortage *alone* is not the
key to the problem of the fall of Rome, and that
any such shortage must be considered against the total
background of all economic and political factors.*

Moses I. Finley

The Question of Population

[Boak's] little book is wholly given
over to arguing a thesis, and the first
response among reviewers and students
has been very favourable. The thesis has
two parts: (1) The population of the
Roman Empire, "never excessive . . ., began to suffer a general decline from the
middle of the second century. This decline in turn created a shortage of manpower which was rendered still more
acute" in the third century. (2) Manpower shortage in its turn was a main
factor in the fall of Rome, defined as
"the gradual disintegration of the Ro-

man Empire in Italy, western Europe,
and north Africa."

Here and there a cautious disclaimer
is dropped into the discussion. Thus,
the possibility is noted that manpower
shortage "might or might not coincide
with, and be the result of, a general
decline in population which would be
defined as depopulation." With similar
caution, Boak writes: "Let me make it
clear . . . that I do not believe there was
any single major cause of this collapse,
but rather a combination of conditions,
forces, and trends which interacted upon

* From review of Boak's *Manpower Shortage* in The *Journal of Roman Studies*, 48
(1958), 156–164. Reprinted by permission of the Society for the Promotion of Roman
Studies, copyright reserved. Page references to Boak's book have been omitted from this
review, together with some of the numerous references to other works, by permission of
M. I. Finley.

one another so that at times it is almost impossible to tell which was cause and which was effect." Nevertheless, the book is so single-minded in its stress on declining population and manpower shortage, that it is fair to ignore the disclaimers and to deal with the bipartite thesis in its bluntest formulation.... Every weakness of the late Empire, even every complaint—*agri deserti*,* the troubles of the curials,† compulsory labour service, army recruitment difficulties, the importation of Germans for military and agricultural purposes, brigandage, poverty, heavy taxation—is directly tied to manpower shortage. Professor Boak is frequently ambiguous about which is cause and which is consequence, and often the connection rests on his bare assertion, but the total effect is always unmistakably in one direction: from manpower shortage to social, political, and economic breakdown.

As a picture of the decline of the western Empire, the book offers a considerable accumulation of data. How valuable a collection it is, or how complete or accurate, need not detain us, because that is not where the importance of the work lies (either in intent or in performance). Admittedly much of the material is well known and accessible in various standard works. What makes the presentation significant is solely the focus. Either Professor Boak has made out a reasonable case for his thesis or he has not: that is the only question to be considered. To do so, it is necessary to examine not only the two parts of his thesis, but also his method.

The prime difficulty which Boak faces is, of course, the lack of figures. His

* "deserted fields"—Ed.
† Local officials—Ed.

opening pages offer a sound and useful reminder that our disability in this respect is total. As he says in a note, "it is quite impossible to calculate with even approximate exactness the population of the city of Rome in ancient times," let alone the population of the Empire or its component regions, or the movements of population. This does not mean that oblique approaches are useless or invalid. Lacking statistics, we must try to get at the problem from other kinds of evidence, which may suggest trends and consequences even though they can never reveal the actual magnitude or rate of population change. Boak rests his case on two interlocking bases: (1) documentary and archaeological evidence which he believes indicates both a declining population and a severe shortage of manpower, and (2) the "known population history of other countries and ... the laws of population trends worked out by specialists in demography." It is this use of the comparative method which requires careful examination before the thesis itself can be tested.

In the West, Boak argues, the declining population trend was "already ... noticeable at the accession of Septimius Severus in 193" and it continued thereafter in a more or less unbroken, accelerating line. His evidence and arguments include: (1) life expectancy figures; (2) analogies from the history of China and medieval England; (3) the failure of the slave population to "maintain itself, much less expand," hence the failure to build up "an internal population pressure"; (4) the general "absence of any population pressures" in the Roman world; (5) "the refusal of the upper and middle classes to raise large families and often even to marry"; (6) the shortage of army recruits;

(7) "the impoverishment which made itself so widely felt"; (8) plague, civil war, and invasions; and (9) the fact that "there is simply no evidence ... for any substantial rise in population after 284." It is obvious that all these arguments, crowded into a dozen octavo pages, are not developed at much length. It is also obvious that, of itself, most of this, even if valid as a picture of the late Roman world, tells us nothing whatever about the size of population or its movement. The heart of the argument is the life-expectancy analysis, without which the author himself would probably place little confidence in the remaining points.

It may be taken as proved that "the duration of life in the Roman Empire corresponded to what is known as the Oriental pattern, illustrated by Egypt, India, and China, and not to the Occidental pattern, found in Italy, France, England, and the United States." But this *is* equally true for the whole of antiquity, and indeed for all pre-industrial society, that is, all of Europe down to the latter half of the eighteenth century and much of the rest of the world into the twentieth century. What follows? "One extremely important result of such studies," says Boak, "is the demonstration that only in the course of the last two centuries have European countries experienced any really great increase in population." This is simply untrue. Boak's authority for the statement, W. F. Willcox, does not say this at all, but only that the great increase in average length of life "has come within the last two centuries." And two pages farther on, Boak himself gives figures purporting to show that the population of England more than trebled between 1086 and 1345. Furthermore, since low life expectancy was a constant

throughout antiquity, it is elementary logic that such a factor cannot explain the downward movements in ancient population if there were also upswings. Boak does not deny that the population within the territory of the Roman Empire was greater at the time of Augustus, let us say, than it had been five centuries earlier. Therefore, unless it can be demonstrated that there was a significant downward change in the life expectancy figures (not just in the population totals) in the later Empire, these figures of themselves are virtually irrelevant. No such demonstration is offered.

Instead, we are given some parallels from medieval England and from China; more precisely, from the views of two scholars, one for each country. The English data are taken exclusively from the work of Josiah Cox Russell, and their authority is by no means unchallenged. ... Indeed, if a recent critique of his methods stands up ... all his calculations and tables simply collapse. And at best, not even Russell's admirers will endorse the "it-has-been-shown" certainty with which Boak adduces his conclusions. For China, Boak rests everything on a short work of Ta Chen, *Population in Modern China* (Chicago 1946 ...). More precisely, Boak rests far more on this book than the author himself claims for it. Elsewhere the latter explains that, for China, "the information now extant is woefully incomplete and generally inaccurate ... the scientific study of China's population problems should no longer be delayed" (*Population Studies* 1, 1947–48, 342). Ta Chen's tentative cyclical theory, even if correct, will not bear the weight Boak puts on it (and it may well be wrong, or at least inadequate ...).

Why China and medieval Britain (and *only* China and medieval Britain) in any event? "In the light of the shortness of life expectancy in the Roman Empire and because of the lack of any evidence of overpopulation, one must conclude that its population pattern conformed to that of medieval and early modern Europe rather than to that of Europe in the last two centuries." That means that more modern western demographic parallels are to be avoided, but it still does not explain the particular choices for comparison, which were made. I am compelled to believe, because they seem to suit the argument. "Periods of any marked increase have been the exception rather than the rule," Boak writes. "It is generally agreed, for example, that in China there has been no material rise in population during the last one hundred years." For this he cites p. 3 of Ta Chen's book, but he fails to indicate that Willcox, the authority for the remark, also estimated that the population of China *had multiplied fivefold* in the preceding two hundred years, 1650–1850. Ta Chen thinks that ratio is too high and he prefers Carr-Saunders' calculation, an increase of 300 per cent, as "more reasonable." Willcox made the further calculation that in the past century, when China's population was stationary, the whole of Asia went up by 300,000,000. . . . A large part of that increase occurred in India, where, according to figures Boak himself gives, life expectancy has been substantially lower than in China.

By basing his whole structure on life expectancy, Boak has managed to give an aura of scientific demography to his otherwise transparently speculative account of the population trend of the later Roman Empire. How successful he has been is seen in the reviews which have already appeared. With only three exceptions that I could discover, the refrain is, "He employs with skill and prudent understanding the methods and results of modern demographic studies. . . ." It is necessary to stress, therefore, that demographers do not pretend to be able to deduce long-term trends from life expectancy figures. For that, they require some way to get at the reproduction rate, and that cannot even be guessed at for antiquity. Low life expectancy obviously restricts the rate of reproduction by the mere fact that a large percentage of women do not live through the entire period in which they are biologically fertile. Given that limit, however, in a stable life-expectancy pattern (whether high or low) the reproduction rate can vary greatly from generation to generation, according to many factors. The argument must proceed from those factors to the population curve, not the other way round.

It is a dangerous illusion to speak, as Boak does, of "the laws of population trends." Modern demography is above all a highly refined technique of statistical analysis. In so far as it has discovered "laws," they are solely in the form, "If all the relevant factors remain unchanged, the present rate of reproduction in a given society will lead to an increase (or decrease) in the population of X per cent in Y years," or of various corollaries that follow from this archetype. Such conclusions result from complex analysis because there is nothing more misleading with respect to population trends than raw census figures, including the raw mortality figures on which Boak lays all his stress. (For the layman, a good introduction on this general point is D. V. Glass, *The Struggle for Population*, Oxford 1936, ch. 1.) No analysis, however, no matter how subtle, permits such a conclusion as this: "Once the birth rate of a people starts to decline, it continues to do so in a geometrical and not merely arithmetical ratio." Demographic laws of so universal and abstract a character simply do not exist. Boak erroneously attributes this "law" to the late Adolphe Landry... by mistaking a simple statistical model for a demographic trend. Moreover, had he read the same page more carefully, he would have found in it a clear statement of the fallacy implicit in the attempt to deduce trends from mere life expectancy figures....

One test case will have to suffice. "Normally," Boak writes, "slave population tends to die out, and Roman slaves were no exception to this rule." His authority is Landry, and what Landry offers, it turns out, is only speculation about the non-fecundity of slaves, without a single piece of evidence. Evidence is available. In the United States, the Negro slave population at the date of the abolition of the slave trade was probably more than double the total number of Negroes imported into the country from the beginning. Hence the natural increase among the slaves was considerable. After the slave trade was abolished, the supply was successfully maintained by breeding. In Jamaica, on the other hand, the slave population never reproduced itself, although it nearly did, once the trade was abolished.... Which of the two is the "normal" pattern? The answer is that there is no universal law of slave population trends, and the lack of evidence regarding Roman slaves cannot be overcome by invoking a "law."....

What follows from all this—with respect to method—is that the use of parallels and analogies requires controls which Boak has failed to exercise. "It is justifiable," he writes "to make use of the known population trends among such peoples in attempting to trace the demographic history of the Roman Empire." By "such peoples" he means, according to the sentence which precedes the one I have quoted, "other peoples living in a comparable cultural atmosphere." I fail to find a single argument in the book which, on this test, warrants the selection of China and medieval England as suitable models for the later Roman Empire. The social, economic, political, and psychological conditions were too different, and hence the premises are lacking for any comparison.

After his opening chapter, Boak proceeds on the assumption that the continuing decline in population is a datum. In discussing the army, for example, he writes: "...as I hope I have demonstrated,...the rural population...was still in process of recession." This is repeated, in one way or another, with reference to the rural population, the urban population, and government services (the three substantive chapters of the book). Then, by what amounts to circular reasoning, he intimates in the summary chapter that his account of *agri deserti,* the curials, and so on, has somehow strengthened the original thesis. It is here at the end, in fact, that he first presents his law of decline in geometric progression. But if there is neither contemporary evidence nor valid comparative arguments for the view in the initial presentation, nothing which follows lends it any support. We may therefore ignore the point hereafter (except incidentally) and turn to the second part of the thesis, the operative role of manpower shortage in the fall of the western Empire. As Boak correctly says, this part of his argument need not stand or fall with the first: in principle, there can be manpower shortage with a stationary, or even a rising, population. . . .

In my examination of Professor Boak's account, I shall take the simple choice he poses at the beginning of the book: "My interest in the problem . . . has been aroused to new activity by the recent suggestion of a prominent historian that there was an acute shortage of manpower from the end of the third century, which was caused, not by a decline in population, but rather by the increased demand for suitable personnel." The reference is to A. H. M. Jones's London inaugural, *Ancient Economic History* (1948). "This is an attractive theory," Boak continues. "I doubt, however, that it can be substantiated." And Boak, as we have seen, proposes the reverse sequence: declining population, hence manpower shortage, hence breakdown. The choice between Jones and Boak, put in this way, is an oversimplification, but it will serve our present concern sufficiently. In making it, I pass no judgment on the ultimate usefulness of Jones's own view of the importance of manpower shortage, even in his limited definition—"the excessive number of idle mouths"; nor do I propose to deny that there had been a drop in numbers from Augustus to Constantine. My sole interest here is in the analytical tool Boak offers us: is it a good one or not?

Army recruitment (to which Boak devotes nearly twenty pages of a total text of only 129 pages) is a fair test. First Boak considers the size of the army and concludes (cautiously and with reserve) that on Diocletian's accession it numbered about 400,000 and that it was increased in the fourth century by about 150,000. These figures, he argues rather

obscurely, imply a new recruiting load on the rural population in the West of "only about 40,000 men in addition to the regular replacements." That requirement was not met easily, for landlords and peasants alike were hostile, the former because they disliked the loss of labour power, the latter because they preferred civilian life. Therefore the emperors resorted to impressment, recruiting of slaves and barbarians, the imposition of hereditary obligations of service upon descendants of veterans. For Professor Boak there is a simple explanation for all this, so obvious that he is content merely to assert it: "Shortage of manpower offers the best explanation of the methods of recruitment employed in the Late Empire."

Boak has apparently overlooked one of the main threads in military history. As G. L. Cheesman phrased it in opening his work on the *auxilia***** (Oxford, 1914, 7): "The extent to which a ruling race can safely use the military resources of its subjects and the effect on both parties of such a relation" is a question "of universal historical interest." The history of armies cannot be separated from the social, economic, and political pattern. Both ruler and ruled have had strong (and not always consistent) views on military service: who bore arms was a very serious matter, the decision involved complex and delicate calculations, and the story cannot be reduced to a simple function of the number of citizens, or inhabitants, or men. More often than not in the past, governments have resorted to the very devices which, when employed by fourth-century Roman emperors, lead Boak to say triumphantly: Here is proof that manpower shortage lay at the root of the evil. If so, the

* Non-Roman troops serving with Roman armies—Ed.

history of armies prior to the nineteenth century (and sometimes beyond) is nothing but a history of manpower shortage —a *reductio ad absurdum*.

In the early eighteenth century, Frederick William I doubled the Prussian military establishment, making it the fourth largest in Europe while his country ranked tenth in territory and thirteenth in population. To accomplish this, "he resorted increasingly to the impressment of his own subjects and to recruiting— . . . at times indistinguishable from kidnapping—in neighbouring states" (Gordon A. Craig, *The Politics of the Prussian Army, 1640–1945,* Oxford, 1955, 8). When this procedure proved inadequate, he shifted to the so-called "canton system," which rested on a principle of universal military obligation with selective service. The army was then composed two thirds of natives, only one third of foreigners. Frederick the Great, however, "set out deliberately to reverse that ratio" and he stated his reason most explicitly: "useful hardworking people should be guarded as the apple of one's eye, and in wartime recruits should be levied in one's own country only when the bitterest necessity compels." The officer corps, on the other hand, was to be purely Prussian; indeed, purely noble Prussian. This transformation came precisely "in a period in which Prussian population and territory were growing." Examples of similar thinking abound in early modern absolutisms. . . . And not only in absolutisms. "The British soldier remained an expensive article whose price advanced despite the growth of population" (Alfred Vagts, *A History of Militarism,* N.Y. 1937, 153). The press gang was a familiar enough feature in English naval recruiting during the Napoleonic Wars, in the very decades when the·population was in-

creasing at a rate unprecedented in the whole of history.

It is the wholesale recruiting of Germans, in particular, upon which Boak places his heaviest stress. This was an "immediate cause of the disintegration of the Western Empire," By itself, this "very fact" of barbarian recruitment reveals the critical manpower shortage, for otherwise such a policy, which was "initiated by Marcus Aurelius" with the Marcomanni, would not have been tolerated. "It cannot be imagined that the imperial government was unaware of the dangers." What the dangers were Boak does not say, nor does he cite texts to justify the view that the emperors (or other contemporaries) believed there were dangers. Presumably the danger is self-evident; it inheres in the word "barbarian" and in their not being "assimilated into the Roman citizen body. A vigorous and expanding population could have absorbed them, but not the enfeebled and discouraged one of the Late Empire." What saved the Eastern emperors was "that they found a source of recruits in the Romanized population of the East with which to counterbalance their Germanic mercenaries.". . .

The most important fact of all is that fourth-century armies, still predominantly composed of recruits from within the Empire, were considerably larger in the over-all than the armies of Augustus and his successors. In other words, the manpower demand upon the population had multiplied. By making light of this increased demand—e.g., *"only* about 40,-000 men" (my italics)—and by stressing the failure to achieve full paper strength, Boak creates the image he seeks. If we take matters in their natural sequence, however, increased demand *preceded* partial failure, and therefore it is reasonable to hold that, other things being

equal, "the recruitment . . . of itself pro-
duce(d) such a critical shortage among
the rural population that its presumed
recovery from the losses of the period
235–84 was checked and instead was
turned into a decline under pressure of
government exactions and regimentation." Yet this view Boak rejects out of
hand. . . .

The mere acknowledgement that there
were significant (and at times even decisive) variables in the picture is sufficient
to undermine Boak's whole structure of
argument. And we have seen that this
is not the only such instance in the book.
It remains to notice one other example,
the most destructive of all. The whole
of Boak's argument, in its details as well
as in its broad sweep, applies equally to
the eastern Empire. He himself notes
that the great plague of 250–270 "probably struck the eastern provinces more
heavily than the western." The chief
devil in the story, the plague of the time
of Marcus Aurelius, may also have orig-
inated in the East. Boak also concedes
that "the West bore a lighter load than
the East in meeting the new (army)
levies." There is good evidence to show
that in the Aegean islands and Asia
Minor, "the registered agricultural population was very thin on the ground according to ancient standards, . . . and
well under half the minimum for efficient cultivation as reckoned by (ancient)
agricultural experts" (A. H. M. Jones,
*JRS** xLiii, 1953, 57). And so on. Yet
the eastern Empire did not "fall." Only
once does Boak face the problem, when
he explains that the eastern emperors
avoided the disaster of a barbarized army
by finding "a source of recruits in the
Romanized population of the East with
which to counterbalance their Germanic

mercenaries." This will not do. If manpower shortage was the key to every
difficulty from the third century on,
including army recruitment, by what
magic were the eastern emperors able
to discover manpower which did not
exist? Stated in general terms, if manpower shortage did not bring down the
eastern Empire, it is not the key to the
fall of the western Empire. (On this
basic problem, see N. H. Baynes, "The
Decline of the Roman Power in Western
Europe: Some Modern Explanations,"
JRS xxxiii, 1943, 29–35; reprinted in his
Byzantine Studies and Other Essays,
London 1955, ch. v.)†

The short of it is that population is
never an independent variable. We can
understand how a severe plague or great
war brings about an immediate reduction, or how improved sanitation and
greater medical knowledge change the
average age of death. But these tell us
nothing about long-term trends. Professor Boak does not seem to have asked
himself what causes a population to rise
or fall over a long period. Apart from
the brief and not very helpful life-expectancy analysis, his account simply assumes some kind of inevitability—in this
instance, inevitably downwards. He is
right to insist that population *is* a factor,
and to protest against the prevailing
indifference among historians of antiquity. That is a service. But with it goes
a danger, that his way of insisting,
and in particular his pretended scientific
laws, will satisfy the longing for neat
solutions. Declining population will then
take the place of soil exhaustion and
race mixture, to become the fashionable
explanation of the '50s and '60s of the
fall of Rome.

English-born EDWARD T. SALMON (1905–   ),
Messecar Professor of History and Principal of
University College at McMaster University, Canada,
approaches the question of population by examining
its connection with the recruitment of the army.
In the following selection he points to a piece of
apparently beneficent legislation—the general
enfranchisement of free men within the Empire—
and suggests that it had the dangerous result of
threatening army recruitment. The prospect of Roman
citizenship had been the "big inducement"
attracting noncitizens into the army.*

Edward T. Salmon

The Roman Army and the Disintegration of the Roman Empire

The popular view that the Roman Empire disappeared owing to a marked change for the worse in the character of the Romans has never found much favour among historians; and it surely must be the case that so *simpliste* a theory cannot possibly be the only explanation. Nevertheless one might well ask whether a change for the worse in a specific part of its population may not have contributed more than a little to the Empire's ultimate disintegration. This is a matter well worth examining, in so far as it concerns the Roman imperial army. In its heyday throughout the first and second centuries A.D. that army was manifestly a magnificent in-strument of power. It met all the basic requirements for a first-class fighting force: an organization careful to the point of elaboration, a singularly efficient system of administration, and a standard of training that enabled it to be victorious in the field. Yet gradually the personnel composing this incomparable force ceased to be respectable elements of the Empire's population. As time went on the army became so barbarized that, by the fifth century and even earlier, the defense of the Empire was quite literally in the hands of Germans; this progressive and accelerating barbarization has long been recognized as an important factor in the so-called

* From *Transactions of the Royal Society of Canada,* Third Series, Section II, 52 (1958),
43–57. Reprinted by permission of the Royal Society of Canada.

"decline and fall." This paper addresses itself to the problem which would appear to be fundamental: the reason for, and the progress of, the barbarization. It is pertinent to ask why the Roman state had recourse to alien defenders; to stress how early this process began; and, above all, to emphasize how Caracalla's enfranchising act, the *Constitutio Antoniniana,* contributed to it.

Over thirty years ago Rostovtzeff insisted that it was really the action of the peasants in making common cause with an undisciplined soldiery to assault the urban bourgeoisie which caused the break-up of the Roman Empire.* This view was clearly coloured by its author's own experiences under the Bolsheviks in his native Russia; today nobody accepts without drastic qualification his picture of a Jacquerie uprising combined with military revolt. It is, in fact, possible to prove that the theory of peasants and soldiery working in a kind of unholy alliance for the extermination of the urban bourgeoisie is very wide of the mark indeed. In the first place, the forces of the Empire, even the Late Empire, were not merely a peasant militia; in the second place, the peasantry suffered just as severely at the hands of the disorderly soldiers as did the city-dwellers. Yet the Russian scholar had done well to emphasize one fact, that in the Roman Empire there was a lack of solidarity between soldiers and civilians.

At least, such was the fact in the chaotic and anarchic third century. But was it equally a fact in the preceding two centuries? When did the rot, so to speak, set in? What caused it?

Tacitus described the scene of Vitellius' legions battling Vespasian's in Rome itself, while "the populace stood by watching the combatants as if at a gladiatorial show, urging on first one side and then the other with their shouts and applause."* From this one is tempted to assume that the split had occurred as early as 69 and that the Roman state was already displaying that fissure which was to put its civilians on one side and its soldiers on another, until ultimately the two elements in the state were completely at loggerheads, if not at daggers drawn. Tacitus himself almost seems to imply as much when he insists that this same unhappy year, 69, revealed the momentous secret of the Empire: that an emperor could be created elsewhere than at Rome. Yet too much ought not to be read into the rhetorical *mot* of the writer who is notoriously the most cynical of all Rome's historians. Nor, possibly, can the behaviour of Rome's civilians be taken as typical. Civilians outside Italy may not have had this attitude of detached indifference to the struggles and aspirations of the soldiers in 69. Troops other than Praetorians simply had no business to be in Rome at all in 69, much less to be converting it into a battleground. Soldiers were stationed in the provinces and should stay where they belonged. Their presence in Rome was contrary to all tradition and practice and as such constituted an offense against its citizens. Under the circumstances one can understand any civilian in Italy, and above all in Rome, adopting an attitude of "a plague on both your houses." Elsewhere in the Empire it may well have been a very different story.

Nor is this all. Except in the year 69—a quite abnormal year which has been given far too much importance—the soldiers were generally well behaved

---

* For Rostovtzeff's views, see pp. 69–75—Ed.

* *Histories,* book 3, chapter 83—Ed.

in the first two centuries. Not until 193 did the legions again rend the Empire asunder with civil war, even though between 69 and 193 there had been occasions when they had had convenient pretexts for doing so. The year 69 is the exception that proves the rule, and even in 69 order was finally re-established, and, once re-established, it remained so for a century and a quarter. Throughout practically the whole of the first two centuries the outlook of the soldiers was not radically different from that of the civilians, a circumstance which is hardly surprising in view of the origins of the legionaries.

The provenance of the Roman soldiers is not altogether unknown despite the almost total failure of the literary sources to refer to it. Authors like Tacitus say very little on the topic, presumably because they could safely assume that their readers would know where the soldiers were mostly recruited. Fortunately, inscriptions have helped to make good the omission. The evidence, regrettably not always datable, consists of such things as soldiers' tombstones, honorific plaques, the few, rare, precious lists of personnel serving in various formations, and the so-called "centurial stones" which help to identify some units and the men serving in them. From the inscriptions it is often possible to tell whether a soldier was an Italian or a provincial either from his birthplace, if that is indicated, or, if it is not, from the citizen tribe in which he (if a legionary) was enrolled, or from the place where the inscription was found. It can be demonstrated that the standing army of the Roman Empire, from the days of Augustus (its founder) onwards, included many non-Italians. These were by no means confined to the *auxilia*:

they, amounting to about half the armed establishment in Augustus' day, were provincial almost to a man; even their officers, although they possessed the Roman citizenship, were often non-Italian. Non-Italians were also present in the legions in large numbers. Today this is a fact familiar to all students of the Empire; but perhaps not everyone realizes that the number of non-Italians was quite certainly very much larger than can be positively proved. For, though many an inscription lists not a soldier's place or origin, but merely his good Italian name, this is no guarantee that he was in fact an Italian: it might merely mean that he was an enfranchised provincial, since it was usual for a provincial to assume an Italian name when he received the Roman citizenship.

The view that the provincialization of the legions did not really begin until Vespasian is no longer tenable. Already in the earliest days of the Empire the process had developed considerably. This may well seem surprising, since it is well known that legionaries, unlike auxiliaries, had to be Roman citizens, and in Augustus' day Roman citizens were still comparatively rare in the provinces. Yet the number of legionaries from the provinces in the first half of the first century was anything but small; in the second half of the same century they were an overwhelming majority; and by the early years of the second century the provincialization of the legions was well-nigh complete. It is clear that the comparatively few Roman citizens in the provinces in Julio-Claudian times could not possibly have supplied all the personnel who were serving in the legions. The conclusion, then, is inescapable: the provincial legionaries, in many cases, must have been given the

Roman citizenship in order to qualify them for service.

If it is true that from the earliest days of the Empire legionaries and auxiliaries alike were recruited from the provinces, one might wonder why certain sons of the provinces were enfranchised and enrolled in the legions, whereas others were not and were assigned to the *auxilia*. Theoretically the recruit's place of origin decided the matter. If he came from a town that was formally organized along municipal lines (in other words, if he possessed *municipalis origo*), he became a legionary; if he came from a country district, then he was required to serve as an auxiliary. In inscriptions, especially those of the first century which are the most likely to indicate a soldier's birthplace, only legionaries appear with *municipalis origo*: an auxiliary is described as hailing from a tribe (*natio*). The reason for this rule was the official conviction that civilization in its best and most veritable form was to be found only in an urban community. Someone from a town could safely be presumed to be ready for Roman citizenship: his assimilation would present no serious difficulties; his outlook could be assumed to be already very similar to that of a native Italian; and consequently he would quickly become imbued with the Roman spirit. The country-dweller, on the other hand, was still in Roman eyes far from civilized; he would not be ready for the citizenship until twenty-five years of service as an auxiliary in the Roman armed forces had familiarized him with Roman ways and the Roman outlook. Thus Greece, completely urbanized and *ex hypothesi* civilized, supplied no *auxilia*, although individuals with Greek names do appear in auxiliary units. Similarly Gallia Narbonensis, a highly urbanized province, provided few auxiliaries, but numerous legionaries. Exactly the reverse was true of the other Gallic provinces, the imperial Tres Galliae: these contained few towns or cities, and in the first two centuries they were in fact the chief recruiting ground for the auxiliary cavalry.

Theory and practice, however, may not always have coincided. What happened, for instance, when not enough men with *municipalis origo* were offering themselves? For it should be remembered that the Roman imperial army was for the most part an army of volunteers. The Roman state, under the Empire as under the Republic, did have the right to conscribe its subjects, citizens or others, for military service. But apparently conscription was not normal under the Empire except in emergencies (cf. *Digest* 49. 16. 4. 10, referring to Trajan's day: *plerumque voluntario milite numeri supplentur*).* In the case of citizens (i.e., potential legionary recruits) conscription seems to have disappeared by Tiberius' reign (14–37); in the case of non-citizens (i.e., potential auxiliary recruits) it continued to be used occasionally. Provincial communities might be allotted quotas and, to fill them, resort to forced levies was sometimes necessary: in such cases the men resented having to serve, especially in areas far from home (Tacitus, *Annals*, 4. 46). On other occasions communities were induced to supply soldiers by tax concessions (Tacitus, *Histories*, 4. 12; *Germ.*, 29). In general, the Roman government would prefer to employ the carrot rather than the stick, since the *auxilia* would be obtained from the martial peoples whom it was dangerous to irritate beyond endurance by ex-

* "normally, the troops are supplied by enlistments"—Ed.

cessive resort to press-gang methods. Other reasons why volunteers should have been preferred readily suggest themselves. The Roman imperial army was a long-service, as well as a standing, force. During the first three centuries twenty-five years was the normal period of service for most soldiers, and clearly it would have been inequitable to use selective conscription to get them. An obvious alternative would have been what used to be called the Continental System (a system of universal conscription and short-term soldiers) and, if Cassius Dio (52. 27) is to be believed, this idea did occur, or was suggested, to Augustus at the time that he was organizing the standing army of the Empire; he deliberately rejected it, Dio implies, on the ground that universal conscription and military training would have been a constant source of public disorder and civil wars. This aspect of the matter may have carried some weight with the canny Augustus. But besides this prudential objection to an army of short-term conscripts, there was another and eminently practical one. The frontiers of the Empire were so far flung that short-service conscripts could scarcely have provided an adequate defense for them. In the days before railways the conscripts would have spent most of their short service careers, not in serious training, but in travelling either to or from their postings; their combat efficiency would not have been very high. The American Civil War proved that in a land of vast distances, even one with railways, short-term troops are not of much use. Accordingly, Augustus and, following his lead, the later emperors decided on an army of long-service troops, usually volunteers.

It is usually argued that there was no particular difficulty in attracting recruits since the numbers involved were small. Legionaries and auxiliaries together amounted to about 300,000 in Augustus' day and could be kept up to strength with an annual intake of 30,000 or less. Is it correct, however, to regard such figures as moderate? An army of 300,000 may seem small by the standards which were set when the Committee of Public Safety of revolutionary France proclaimed universal conscription in 1793, but by the standards of the ancients it was prodigious. The Hellenistic monarchies, the Roman Republic, the state of Parthia would all have regarded such a force as formidable if not staggering.

In view of the conditions of service difficulties in recruitment would hardly be surprising. The serving soldier had a rough time. The pay for a man in the legions in the first two centuries was low, less than a *denarius* a day; and his "take home" pay was lower still, for apparently he had to pay for his personal weapons, his clothing, his rations, and even his tent. The man in the *auxilia* must have been even worse off, the best proof being that an interservice transfer (*militiae mutatio*), from legions to *auxilia*, was the prescribed punishment for certain military offences. Moreover, discipline was harsh; even in the legions corporal punishment, arbitrarily inflicted, was normal, and fatigue duties were so onerous that the soldier spent a good deal of his meagre pay bribing his way out of them. True, he came in for the occasional windfall in the shape of a donative or a share in war-booty, although what Pliny calls the *immensa maiestas pacis Romanae** meant that he could not hope for very much of the latter; and of course on discharge he

* "the vast majesty of the Roman peace"—Ed

was entitled to a gratuity, which, however, sometimes failed to materialize and in any case could hardly be described as princely. Nor was there much glamorous excitement to compensate for the tough service conditions. Service life was passed in a frontier province far from the amusements and the amenities of a city like Rome, and when, early in the second century, Hadrian abandoned Trajan's dynamic policy the soldier's life was only too likely to consist of little more than boring and morale-shattering guard duty in an immobile unit. Legally he could not even marry: prior to the third century his partner, if any, had the legal status of a concubine and his children, if any, were legally SP (*sine patre*).*

Manifestly there was not much to attract volunteers, and indeed it was no simple matter to keep the numbers of such a redoubtable force up to strength from the ranks of Roman citizens only. In the first century the numbers could sometimes only be maintained by obliging veterans whose time had expired to continue with the colours. The astonishing thing is that nevertheless such volunteers as were forthcoming in the first two centuries included quite a large proportion of the Empire's better classes. Inscriptions prove that many of the provincial legionaries came from good, middle-class families and were men of excellent education and superior intelligence. Many of them were good officer material and rose from the ranks to become centurions, and it may have been the prospect of such promotion that caused some of them to enlist; but since it was normally reserved for those provincials whose Roman citizenship was of fairly long standing (and there were few

* "without a father"—Ed.

of these), it is safe to assume that it was not the prospect of becoming officers that attracted many of the better class provincial recruits into the army.

The prospect of Roman citizenship was the big inducement. Roman citizenship improved the social standing, but above all the civil status, of the recipient; it opened far more opportunities for him and his family. All provincials were eager to acquire it, and there was virtually only one avenue to it: service in the Roman imperial army. If provincials served in the legions they obtained the citizenship the moment they enlisted; if they served in the *auxilia* they obtained it twenty-five years later on their release from service. It was this desire of the provincials to acquire Roman citizenship that accounts for the fact that during the first two centuries voluntary enlistments sufficed to keep the armed services up to establishment.

Certainly the army would not have remained at full strength if it had depended on volunteers from those who already possessed the Roman citizenship. For these showed a most remarkable disinclination to serve. The rigours of service life no doubt help to account for the Roman citizen's aversion; but there was probably another reason as well. Examples of countries where the service conditions are hardly any better than in the Roman Empire but which nevertheless have had comparatively little difficulty in inducing men to join up can be adduced. Patriotism is the spur. If patriotism did not similarly inspire "the man in the Roman street," to use Mattingly's phrase, it must have been largely because the régime of the Caesars was an authoritarian régime, a benevolently paternalist one at times perhaps, but authoritarian for all that, one in which the man in the street was not only not encouraged to participate in public life but was positively dissuaded from doing so. He had no share in affairs of state, which were exclusively the domain of his betters. He naturally had no voice in any decision, since it was the *sapientissimus et unus,* the emperor, who decided everything. The average citizen was not even regularly and systematically informed about public affairs and imperial policies, for in the Roman Empire there was no system of universal state education nor even a popular press. All that the average citizen really knew was that he belonged to an Empire that was certainly mighty and apparently invincible and that he was expected to leave its administration to others. Is it any wonder that the fires of patriotism burned low? The average citizen could hardly be blamed for assuming that the Empire had no desperate need for him. His services were obviously not desired for helping to run the Empire, and in view of its seeming impregnability they did not appear to be very much needed for helping to defend it either. As Mommsen pointed out many years ago, Augustus' achievement in re-establishing law and order and providing the world with peace and a *princeps* relieved the average Roman citizen of any responsibility in that regard. The average Roman citizen forthwith concluded that he was entitled to escape military service. Exemption from military service, in fact, came to be regarded as one of the privileges to which the *ingenuus,* the Roman citizen born, was entitled.

In Italy, where of course virtually all who were not slaves were citizens, recruits were notoriously hard to find. When, at the time of the Pannonian Revolt and the Teutoburg Disaster, Augustus suddenly and urgently needed men, he found himself obliged to enlist freedmen and even slaves in the legions. His successor, Tiberius, deplored the Italian aversion for military service but could not correct it. Shortly after the middle of the first century legions could be described as *militem peregrinum et externum,** and by 100 they could be referred to as the *militia provincialis.* By 100, then, serious attempts to recruit legionaries in Italy had been abandoned, and, even though there were still perhaps some Italians serving in the legions in the second century, most of them who had any hankering for the military life were much more likely to be found in the Praetorian Guards.

Roman citizens in the provinces, especially in the armed, imperial provinces, may have come forward in somewhat larger numbers than did Roman citizens in Italy. It was often a case of a son following his father's profession. A soldier who passed his service life in a frontier province often settled down there on his discharge. If he settled near the frontier instead of deep inside the province, there might well be very few avenues to employment, apart from the army, for his son, whose lifetime familiarity with the army might give him some advantage over other recruits. It is significant that numerous inscriptions, many of them later than 100, record soldiers as having been born *castris;* that is, in the settlement (*canabae*) that sprang up around a garrison on the frontier. Yet by no means every son followed his father into the army. The literature of the Empire reveals that, even in the provinces, the man who already possessed Roman citizenship was usually reluctant to become a soldier.

* "foreign and alien soldiery"—Ed.

Indeed it almost looks as if citizenship implied exemption from military service, and it is probably not so very wide of the mark to suggest that this was one of the things that made citizenship so desirable.

Now it is obvious that in the provinces the number of Roman citizens was ever increasing, for not only the legionaries and, on their discharge, the auxiliaries, but also their offspring acquired citizenship; this is a matter of the utmost consequence. For if it was the prize of citizenship that attracted men into the army, then clearly the law of diminishing returns was bound, sooner or later, to apply: the more widespread the citizenship, the more restricted the area from which recruits were likely to be obtained. In particular the towns and cities, a steadily increasing number of which acquired the status of Roman *municipia* or even obtained the charters of *coloniae*,* failed to produce their quota of recruits. When the legions could not be kept up to strength from the urban centres their ranks necessarily had to be filled from the country district. Authenticated instances of legionaries whose ostensible *municipalis origo* is clearly fictitious and was invented for them merely to qualify them for legionary service can be found as early as the first century in the eastern half of the Empire. In the second century the practice became universal, so that gradually the distinction between legionary and auxiliary recruits disappeared; both alike were being obtained from the country districts and, increasingly, from the country districts near the frontiers. This fact may explain why, after 138, the children of an auxiliary

* *Coloniae,* "colonies," were towns of Roman citizens and ranked above *municipia*, "towns"— Ed.

were no longer granted the citizenship along with their father on the latter's release from service. Here we probably have an attempt to preserve at least one good source of volunteers. For, as we have seen, even though soldiers' sons might be more likely prospects for the army than other elements in the population, they too lost their willingness to volunteer the moment that they became citizens. So they were kept in the status of non-citizens for as long as possible: after 138, the auxiliary on discharge acquired the citizenship for himself alone; if his son wanted it, then like his father before him he had to serve in the army to get it.

The effect of the continuous contraction of the recruiting areas must have been most marked on the *auxilia*. For if the citizenship was the big inducement, then obviously men would prefer to join the service which gave it to them immediately on enlistment. In other words, the legions were bound to get the pick of the provincial recruits, leaving only the dregs for the *auxilia*. In fact, special inducements had to be offered. It is to be noted that, from the beginning of the second century, an increasing number of auxiliaries were Roman citizens even before their discharge (a recent calculation estimates that well before the end of the century almost half of them were in this category); evidently, for the *auxilia* no less than for the legions, the citizenship was being used as a bribe: it may have been given on enlistment or, more probably, special facilities may have been devised for auxiliaries to acquire it. But despite this the human material in the *auxilia* was anything but the best. Good evidence of this is the emergence *c.* 100, and the increasing importance thereafter, of a new type of *auxilia,* the national *numeri.* As compared with other auxiliaries, these were looser in organization and more barbarous in character (the titles of the units suggest that they were drawn from the most uncivilized districts of the Empire), and as the second century wore on ever greater use was made of these barbarian irregulars. By the late second century better-class provincials without the citizenship must have been very few; and consequently the difficulty of obtaining really desirable recruits is hardly surprising. Instead of being men of good family the recruits were now only too likely to be drawn from the lowest and most primitive elements. Throughout the first and a large part of the second century the recruits' motive had been, if not exactly patriotic, at least not discreditable (for there was nothing inherently unworthy in the desire to acquire Roman citizenship), but it now became worse than dubious. Recruits were only too apt to be men of the rough and reckless type, who were joining the army chiefly in order to get weapons in their hands with which they would be able to extort for themselves an ever greater share of the Empire's collective wealth. Possibly at first they had no clear conception that they were in fact preying upon organized society, and no doubt it took some time before the size and frequency of their demands spelled complete economic ruin for the Empire. Yet already under the first emperor of the third century, Septimius Severus, who, as a provincial born without a drop of Italian blood in his veins, symbolizes in his own person the spread of the citizenship, the soldiers had to be humoured. His army, according to an eye-witness, was a motley throng very savage to see, very fearsome to hear, and very uncouth to approach. Severus, significantly, thought it necessary to advise his son and successor to enrich the soldiers and disregard everybody else.

If things had reached this pass by *c.* 200, what was likely to be the state of affairs after 212, when Caracalla's *Constitutio Antoniniana* enfranchised all the freeborn inhabitants of the Empire regardless of their race, origin, creed, or mother-tongue? Whatever Caracalla's principal motive may have been, one effect must have been to eliminate what had been a prime inducement for men to enlist. Henceforth it would become increasingly necessary to go outside the Empire altogether in search of soldiers. The thesis of this paper is the tragic paradox that what can surely be regarded as one of the more enlightened features of the Roman Empire, the liberality with which it bestowed its citizenship, contributed in no small measure to its downfall by completing the ruin of the Roman imperial army.

After 212 the army was only too often at odds with the civilians. Cassius Dio, who became consul at Rome within a few years of Caracalla's enfranchising act, took it for granted that an army of long-term volunteers would consist of that "most vigorous but violent element in the population which is usually obliged to make its living by banditry."[*] The Roman imperial army, like any other, had always included a certain proportion of adventurous roughnecks, and even of criminals, in its ranks. But so long as the prospect of acquiring Roman citizenship had spurred men of a different stamp to enlist, it had not got out of hand. In the third century, however, it became quite uncontrollable. It kindled an unending series of civil wars,

[*] Cassius Dio 52. 27.

it spawned a well-nigh inexhaustible list of pretenders, it made and unmade emperors with the most reckless abandon, and it battened greedily on everything that it could extort from the civilian population. This parlous state of affairs, significantly, supervened after 212 when there were to all intents and purposes no non-citizens left in the Empire. It is with Maximin (235–8) that the anarchy of the so-called Barrack Emperors really begins.

It would not have been easy in any case to maintain the army at full strength because of the way that the population of the Empire, or at least of its western half, was beginning to decline. In the west a serious shortage of manpower, caused possibly by epidemics, possibly by excessive urbanization (cities being notoriously bad breeders), possibly by other factors, was starting to manifest itself. This, of course, aggravated the problem of finding recruits. Changed conditions of warfare also no doubt complicated recruiting. As cavalry came to play an ever more important role, the wild cowboys of the frontier areas would be in demand. But probably it was not so much the decline in population or the need for skilled riders as the universal grant of citizenship that was responsible for the deterioration in army personnel. Men of the better type no longer had any inducement to volunteer.

With the citizenship no longer available as a bribe, various devices were used to attract recruits: increased pay, free rations, larger and more frequent donatives, the right to legal wedlock. Severus Alexander is said to have offered grants of land as the bait to soldiers' sons. But it was all to no avail: none of these makeshifts improved the calibre of the troops. When, towards the end of the third century, barbarian assaults had helped to rekindle the fires of patriotism, it might be another story; for the time being, that is, for the middle years of the third century, the Roman army did not get enough recruits and those that it did get were *faute de mieux* obtained for the most part from the roughest and lowest elements of the population, if not from the martial peoples outside the Empire, men who knew little and cared less about Rome's mission and who, when not preying upon the civilians, had not the slightest compunction about preying upon one another.

It was the chaos caused by these unruly soldiers which provided the barbarians beyond the frontiers with their opportunity, and they seized it with avidity. And the assaults of these barbarian hordes led directly to the most obvious, if not indeed the most important, of all the causes for the decline and fall: military collapse.

Surely, however, the historian's duty is to explain, if he can, why the barbarians attacked in the first place and why they were so successful when they did. It may not be fanciful to seek the explanation in the reduced numbers, and above all in the inferior character, of the men in the ranks of the Roman imperial army in the third century, an army which, owing to Caracalla's enfranchising act, was probably undermanned and recruited largely from the irresponsible elements of the population. An Empire whose defenders were thus few in quantity and poor in quality must have been tempting bait to the outer barbarians. Small wonder is it that they fell upon the Empire and thereby set in train that fateful sequence of events which resulted finally in its disintegration.

TENNEY FRANK (1876–1939) was professor of Latin
at Johns Hopkins University and one of America's
most renowned Roman historians. His special field
was economic history; he organized and edited
An Economic Survey of Ancient Rome (Baltimore,
1933–1940) and himself wrote *An Economic History
of Rome* (Baltimore, 2d ed., 1927) as well as other
books on Roman history and literature. The
article reprinted here seeks to prove a high degree
of "racial" mixture in Rome from names on
tombstones and other inscriptions.*

Tenney Frank

Race Mixture in the Roman Empire

There is one surprise that the historian usually experiences upon his first visit to Rome. It may be at the Galleria Lapidaria of the Vatican or at the Lateran Museum, but, if not elsewhere, it can hardly escape him upon his first walk up the Appian Way. As he stops to decipher the names upon the old tombs that line the road, hoping to chance upon one familiar to him from his Cicero or Livy, he finds praenomen and nomen promising enough, but the cognomina all seem awry. L. Lucretius *Pamphilus*, A. Aemilius *Alexa*, M. Clodius *Philostorgus* do not smack of freshman Latin. And he will not readily find in the Roman writers now extant an answer to the questions that these inscriptions invariably raise. Do these names imply that the Roman stock was completely changed after Cicero's day, and was the satirist recording a fact when he wailed that the Tiber had captured the waters of the Syrian Orontes? If so, are these foreigners ordinary immigrants, or did Rome become a nation of ex-slaves and their offspring? Or does the abundance of Greek cognomina mean that, to a certain extent, a foreign nomenclature has gained respect, so that a Roman dignitary might, so to speak, sign a name like C. Julius Abascantus on the hotel register without any misgivings about the accommodations?

Unfortunately, most of the sociological and political data of the empire are pro-

* From the *American Historical Review*, 21 (1915–1916), 689-708. Reprinted by permission of the American Historical Association.

vided by satirists. When Tacitus informs us that in Nero's day a great many of Rome's senators and knights were descendants of slaves and that the native stock had dwindled to surprisingly small proportions, we are not sure whether we are not to take it as an exaggerated thrust by an indignant Roman of the old stock. At any rate, this, like similar remarks equally indirect, receives totally different evaluation in the discussion of those who have treated of Rome's society, like Friedländer, Dill, Mommsen, Wallon, and Marquardt. To discover some new light upon these fundamental questions of Roman history, I have tried to gather such fragmentary data as the corpus of inscriptions might afford. This evidence is never decisive in its purport, and it is always, by the very nature of the material, partial in its scope, but at any rate it may help us to interpret our literary sources to some extent. It has at least convinced me that Juvenal and Tacitus were not exaggerating. It is probable that when these men wrote a very small percentage of the free plebeians on the streets of Rome could prove unmixed Italian descent. By far the larger part—perhaps ninety per cent— had Oriental blood in their veins.

My first quest was for information about the stock of the ordinary citizen of Rome during the empire. In the *Corpus of Latin Inscriptions* the editors, after publishing the honorary and sepulchral inscriptions of the nobles and military classes, followed by those of the slaves and humble classes which occur in the *columbaria*,* gave the rest of the city's sepulchral inscriptions (19,260) in alphabetical order. Of these I read the 13,900 contained in volume VI, parts 2 and 3, which, despite the occurrence of

* Subterranean sepulchres—Ed.

some slaves as well as of some persons of wealth, represent on the whole the ordinary type of urban plebeians. A mere classification of all these names into lists of natives on the one hand and slaves and foreigners on the other would be of little service, since, obviously, transient foreigners are of little importance in estimating the stock of the permanent population of Rome, and we must face the question at once whether or not the slave and freedman stock permanently merged into the civil population. Furthermore, such lists will be at everyone's hand as soon as the index of the sixth volume of *CIL.* is published. In reckoning up the foreign stock, therefore, I have counted only those who, according to the inscriptions, were presumably born at Rome. A somewhat arbitrary definition of limits was necessary since we are seldom given definite information about the place of birth, but as I have used the same classification for the free-born as for the slave-born the results are valid for our purposes. For instance, in getting statistics of birth, I have included all children under ten years of age, assuming that slave children under that age would rarely be brought in from abroad; and if slaves of this class are counted, the free-born of the same class must also be reckoned with. I have also included slave and free-born children who appear to be with father, mother, brother, or sister at Rome, since presumably they would have been sundered from their family if they had been brought in from the foreign market; and again, in order to reach fair results, the corresponding persons of free birth are counted. For reasons which will presently appear I have accepted the Greek cognomen as a true indication of recent foreign extraction, and, since citizens of native stock did not as a rule unite in marriage with *liberti*,* a Greek cognomen in a child or one parent is sufficient evidence of status. As is well known, certain Latin cognomina, *e.g.*, Salvius, Hilarus, Fortunatus, were so frequently borne by slaves and freedmen that they were apt to be avoided by the better classes. Nevertheless, since no definite rule is attainable in the matter, I have credited the bearers of all Latin names to the native stock in all cases of doubt.

Classifying in this way the names of the aforesaid 13,900 inscriptions of volume VI., parts 2 and 3, we find that of the 4485 persons apparently born at Rome, 3723 (eighty-three per cent.) fall into the list which by our criteria represents foreign extraction. This figure is probably not far from correct, but I think it would be raised somewhat if it were possible to decide what proportion of Latin cognomina conceals slaves and *liberti*. For instance, a name like Q. Manlius Restitutus (VI. 22015) would usually pass with little suspicion. But the inscription also names his father, mother, wife and two sons, all of whom have Greek cognomina. Because of his parentage I have classed him as of foreign stock, but there are scores of brief inscriptions in which the necessary facts are not provided. In these the subject had to be classed, however erroneously, as Latin.

Who are these Romans of the new type and whence do they come? How many are immigrants, and how many are of servile extraction? Of what race are they? . . .

. . . It may well be that many of the ex-slave rabble who spoke the languages of the East imposed upon the uncritical by passing as free-born immigrants. Even freedmen were not beyond pretending that they had voluntarily chosen slavery as a means of attaining to Roman citizenship by way of the *vindicta*.† At any rate, the Roman inscriptions have very few records of free-born foreigners. Such men, unless they attained to citizenship, ought to bear names like that in no. 17171, *Dis man. Epaeneti, Epaeneti F. Ephesio,* but there are not a dozen names of this sort to be found among the inscriptions of volume VI., parts 2 and 3. Nor need we assume that many persons of this kind are concealed among the inscriptions that bear the *tria nomina*,** for immigrants of this class did not often perform the services for which the state granted citizenship. There could hardly have been an influx of foreign free-born laborers at Rome, for Rome was not an industrial city and was more than well provided with poor citizens who could not compete with slaves and had to live upon the state's bounty. Indeed, an examination of the laborious article by Kühn fails to reveal any free-born foreigners among the skilled laborers of the city. In regard to shop-keepers, merchants, and traders we may refer to a careful discussion by Pârvan. He has convincingly shown that the retail trade was carried on at Rome, not by foreigners but by Romans of the lower classes, mostly slaves and freedmen, and that while the provincials of Asia and Egypt continued throughout the empire to carry most of the imports of the East to Rome, the Roman houses had charge of the wholesale trade in the city. The free-born foreigner did not make any inroad upon this field. However, in various arts and crafts, such as those

* Freed slaves—Ed.

† The rod with which a slave was touched when being freed—Ed.

** The "three names" commonly possessed by Roman citizens—Ed.

mentioned by Juvenal, the free immigrant could gain a livelihood at Rome. Some of the teachers of rhetoric, philosophy, and mathematics, some of the doctors, sculptors, architects, painters, and the like, were citizens of the provincial cities who went to Rome for greater remuneration. But even most of these professions were in the hands of slaves and freedmen who had been given a specialized education by their masters. In volume VI., part 2, which contains the sepulchral inscriptions classified according to arts and crafts, there is very little trace of the free-born foreigner. Among the fifty inscriptions of *medici,* for instance, only two, 9563, 9597, contain sure instances of such foreigners. Among the *grammatici, rhetores, argentarii, structores,* and *pictores,** where they might well be expected, I find no clear case. It is evident then that the sweeping statements of men like Juvenal and Seneca should not be made the basis for assuming a considerable free-born immigration that permanently altered the citizen-body of Rome. These writers apparently did not attempt to discriminate between the various classes that were speaking foreign jargons on the streets of Rome. As a matter of fact, this foreign-speaking population had, for the most part, it seems, learned the languages they used within the city itself from slaves and freedman parents of foreign birth. . . .

But however numerous the offspring of the servile classes, unless the Romans had been liberal in the practice of manumission, these people would not have merged with the civil population. Now, literary and legal records present abundant evidence of an unusual liberality

* Schoolteachers, rhetoricians, bankers, carpenters, painters—Ed.

in this practice at Rome, and the facts need not be repeated after the full discussions of Wallon, Buckland, Friedländer, Dill, Lemonnier, and Cicotti. If there were any doubt that the laws passed in the early empire for the partial restriction of manumission did not seriously check the practice, the statistics given at the beginning of the paper would allay it. When from eighty to ninety per cent of the urban-born population proves to have been of servile extraction, we can only conclude that manumission was not seriously restricted. I may add that a count of all the slaves and freedmen in the *familiae* of the aristocratic households mentioned above showed that almost a half were *liberti.* It is difficult to believe that this proportion represents the usual practice, however, and, in fact, the figures must be used with caution. On the one hand, they may be too high, for many who served as slaves all their lives were manumitted only in old age, and it must also be recognized that slaves were less apt to be recorded than *liberti.* On the other hand, the figures may in some respects be too low, since there can be little doubt that the designation *liberti* was at times omitted on the simple urns, even though the subject had won his freedom. However, as far as the inscriptions furnish definite evidence, they tell the same tale as the writers of Rome, namely, that slaves were at all times emancipated in great numbers.

When we consider whence these slaves came and of what stock they actually were, we may derive some aid from an essay by Bang, *Die Herkunft der Römischen Sklaven.* Bang has collected all the inscriptions like *Damas, natione Syrus,* and *C. Ducenius C. lib. natus in Syria,* which reveal the provenance of slaves.

Of course, the number of inscriptions giving such information is relatively small, a few hundred in all. It should also be noticed that when a slave gives his nationality he shows a certain pride in it, which, in some cases at least, implies that he is not a normal slave of the mart, born in servitude, but rather a man of free birth who may have come into the trade by capture, abduction, or some other special way. However, with this word of caution we may use Bang's statistics for what they are worth.

A very large proportion in his list (seven-eighths of those dating in our era) came from within the boundaries of the empire. From this we may possibly infer that war-captives were comparatively rare during the empire, and that, though abduction and kidnapping supplied some of the trade, the large bulk of the slaves were actually reared from slave-parents. Doubtless slaves were reared with a view to profit in Greece and the Orient, as well as in Italy, and I see no reason for supposing that the situation there differed much from that of our Southern States where—for obvious economic reasons—the birth-rate of slaves was higher between 1800 and 1860 than the birth-rate of their free descendants has been since then. An examination of the names in Bang's list with reference to the provenance of the bearer will do something toward giving a criterion for judging the source of Italian slaves not otherwise specified. In a very few cases a name appears which is not Greek or Latin but Semitic, Celtic, etc., according to the birthplace of the slave, as, for instance, Malchio, Zizas, Belatusa. Such names are rare and never cause any difficulty. Somewhat more numerous, and equally clear of interpretation, are the generic names that explicitly give the race of the bearer, like Syrus, Cappadox, Gallus, etc. In general, however, slaves have Greek or Latin names, and here difficulties arise, for it has by no means been certain whether or not these names had so distinctively a servile a connotation that they might be applied indiscriminately to captives from the North and West, as well as to the slaves of Italy and the East. Nevertheless, there seems to be a fairly uniform practice which differentiated between Greek and Latin names during the empire. Slaves from Greece, from Syria, from Asia Minor, including the province of Asia, Phrygia, Caria, Lycia, Pamphylia, Cappadocia, Bithynia, Paphlagonia, Galatia—that is, from regions where Greek was the language of commerce, regularly bore Greek, rather than Latin, names. Slaves from the North—from Germany to Dacia —as a rule bore Latin names. Presumably their own barbaric names were difficult to pronounce and Greek ones seemed inappropriate. Slaves from Spain and Gaul bore Latin and Greek names in about equal number. But here we must apparently discriminate. These provinces were old and commerce had brought into them many Oriental slaves from the market. It may be that the Greek names were applied mostly to slaves of Eastern extraction. This I should judge to be the case at least with the following: Ephesia (Bang, p. 239), Corinthus, Hyginus, Phoebus (his father's name is Greek), Eros (a *Sevir Aug.*),* and Philocyrius. . . . In general we may apply these criteria in trying in some measure to decide the provenance of slaves in Italy whose nativity is not specified: bearers of Greek names are in general from the East or descendants of Eastern slaves who have been in the West;

* A type of Roman priest—Ed.

bearers of Latin names are partly captives of the North and West, partly, as we have seen from our Roman lists, Easterners and descendants of Easterners who have received Latin names from their masters.

Therefore, when the urban inscriptions show that seventy per cent of the city slaves and freedmen bear Greek names and that a large proportion of the children who have Latin names have parents of Greek names, this at once implies that the East was the source of most of them, and with that inference Bang's conclusions entirely agree. In his list of slaves that specify their origin as being outside of Italy (during the empire), by far the larger portion came from the Orient, especially from Syria and the provinces of Asia Minor, with some from Egypt and Africa (which for racial classification may be taken with the Orient). Some are from Spain and Gaul, but a considerable proportion of these came originally from the East. Very few slaves are recorded from the Alpine and Danube provinces, while Germans rarely appear, except among the imperial bodyguard. Bang remarks that Europeans were of greater service to the empire as soldiers than as servants. This is largely true, but, as Strack has commented, the more robust European war-captives were apt to be chosen for the gruelling work in the mines and in industry, and consequently they have largely vanished from the records. Such slaves were probably also the least productive of the class; and this, in turn, helps to explain the strikingly Oriental aspect of the new population. . . .

There are other questions that enter into the problem of change of race at Rome, for the solution of which it is even more difficult to obtain statistics.

For instance, one asks, without hope of a sufficient answer, why the native stock did not better hold its own. Yet there are at hand not a few reasons. We know for instance that when Italy had been devasted by Hannibal and a large part of its population put to the sword, immense bodies of slaves were bought up in the East to fill the void; and that during the second century, when the plantation system with its slave service was coming into vogue, the natives were pushed out of the small farms and many disappeared to the provinces of the ever-expanding empire. Thus, during the thirty years before Tiberius Gracchus, the census statistics show no increase. During the first century B.C., the importation of captives and slaves continued, while the free-born citizens were being wasted in the social, Sullan, and civil wars. Augustus affirms that he had had half a million citizens under arms, one-eighth of Rome's citizens, and that the most vigorous part. During the early empire, twenty to thirty legions, drawn of course from the best free stock, spent their twenty years of vigor in garrison duty, while the slaves, exempt from such services, lived at home and increased in number. In other words, the native stock was supported by less than a normal birth-rate, whereas the stock of foreign extraction had not only a fairly normal birth-rate but a liberal quota of manumissions to its advantage. . . .

But the existence of other forms of "race suicide", so freely gossipped about by writers of the empire, also enters into this question, and here the inscriptions quite fail us. The importance of this consideration must, nevertheless, be kept in mind. Doubtless, as Fustel de Coulanges (*La Cité Antique*) has remarked, it could have been of little importance in the society of the republic so long as the old orthodox faith in ancestral spirits survived, for the happiness of the *manes** depended upon the survival of the family, and this religious incentive probably played the same rôle in the propagation of the race as the Mosaic injunctions among the Hebrews, which so impressed Tacitus in a more degenerate day of Rome. But religious considerations and customs—which in this matter emanate from the fundamental instincts that continue the race—were questioned as all else was questioned before Augustus's day. Then the process of diminution began. The significance of this whole question lies in the fact that "race suicide" then, as now, curtailed the stock of the more sophisticated, that is, of the aristocracy and the rich, who were, to a large extent, the native stock. Juvenal, satirist though he is, may be giving a fact of some social importance when he writes that the poor bore all the burdens of family life, while the rich remained childless:

jacet aurato vix ulla puerpera lecto;
Tantum artes hujus, tantum medicamina
possunt,
Quae steriles facit.†

There may lie here—rare phenomenon —an historic parallel of some meaning. The race of the human animal survives by means of instincts that shaped themselves for that purpose long before rational control came into play. Before our day it has only been at Greece and Rome that these impulses have had to face the obstacle of sophistication. There at least the instinct was beaten, and the

race went under. The legislation of Augustus and his successors, while aimed at preserving the native stock, was of the myopic kind so usual in social lawmaking, and, failing to reckon with the real nature of the problem involved, it utterly missed the mark. By combining epigraphical and literary references, a fairly full history of the noble families can be procured, and this reveals a startling inability of such families to perpetuate themselves. We know, for instance, in Caesar's day of forty-five patricians, only one of whom is represented by posterity when Hadrian came to power. The Aemilii, Fabii, Claudii, Manlii, Valerii, and all the rest, with the exception of the Cornelii, have disappeared. Augustus and Claudius raised twenty-five families to the patriciate, and all but six of them disappear before Nerva's reign. Of the families of nearly four hundred senators recorded in 65 A.D. under Nero, all trace of a half is lost by Nerva's day, a generation later. And the records are so full that these statistics may be assumed to represent with a fair degree of accuracy the disappearance of the male stock of the families in question. Of course members of the aristocracy were the chief sufferers from the tyranny of the first century, but this havoc was not all wrought by *delatores*** and assassins. The voluntary choice of childlessness accounts largely for the unparalleled condition. This is as far as the records help upon this problem, which, despite the silence, is probably the most important phase of the whole question of the change of race. Be the causes what they may, the rapid decrease of the old aristocracy and the native stock was clearly concomitant with a twofold increase from below: by a more normal

* Spirits of the dead—Ed.
† "Scarcely any woman gives birth on a gilded bed; so effective are the skills of the abortionist and such is the power of her drugs": Juvenal, *Satires,* 6.594–596—Ed.

** Professional accusers—Ed.

birth-rate of the poor, and the constant manumission of slaves.

This Orientalizing of Rome's populace has a more important bearing than is usually accorded it upon the larger question of why the spirit and acts of imperial Rome are totally different from those of the republic, if indeed racial characteristics are not wholly a myth. There is to-day a healthy activity in the study of the economic factors—unscientific finance, fiscal agriculture, inadequate support of industry and commerce, etc.—that contributed to Rome's decline. But what lay behind and constantly reacted upon all such causes of Rome's disintegration was, after all, to a considerable extent, the fact that the people who built Rome had given way to a different race. The lack of energy and enterprise, the failure of foresight and common sense, the weakening of moral and political stamina, all were concomitant with the gradual diminution of the stock which, during the earlier days, had displayed these qualities. It would be wholly unfair to pass judgment upon the native qualities of the Orientals without a further study, or to accept the self-complacent slurs of the Romans, who, ignoring certain imaginative and artistic qualities, chose only to see in them unprincipled and servile egoists. We may even admit that had the new races had time to amalgamate and attain a political consciousness, a more brilliant and versatile civilization might have come to

birth. That, however, is not the question. It is apparent that at least the political and moral qualities which counted most in the building of the Italian federation, the army organization, the provincial administrative system of the republic, were the qualities most needed in holding the empire together. And however brilliant the endowment of the new citizens, these qualities they lacked. The Trimalchios* of the empire were often shrewd and daring business men, but their first and obvious task apparently was to climb by the ladder of quick profits to a social position in which their children with Romanized names could comfortably proceed to forget their forebears. The possession of wealth did not, as in the republic, suggest certain duties toward the commonwealth. Narcissus and Pallas might be sagacious politicians, but they were not expected to be statesmen concerned with the continuity of the *mos majorum.*† And when, on reading Tacitus, we are amazed at the new servility of Scipios and Messallas, we must recall that these scattered inheritors of the old aristocratic ideals had at their back only an alien rabble of ex-slaves, to whom they would have appealed in vain for a return to ancestral ideas of law and order. They had little choice between servility and suicide, and not a few chose the latter.

* Trimalchio is a vulgar and ostentatious freedman in Petronius' novel, the *Satyricon*—Ed.

† "ancestral custom," a favorite political slogan in Rome—Ed.

S. COLUM GILFILLAN (1889–   ) taught at several American colleges and was for many years a research associate at the University of Chicago, where he worked especially on prediction. Among his books are *The Sociology of Invention* (1935) and *Social Implications of Technical Advance* (1953). In this excerpt he exposes the fact that many Romans suffered from lead poisoning and draws conclusions about the unwitting extermination of the upper class.*

S. Colum Gilfillan

Roman Culture and Dysgenic Lead Poisoning

Our novel theory concerns what mattered most about the fall of Rome. This was not the empire's military defeat and break-up—those might even have been benefits to mankind. What concerns us most is the *decay* of Rome, the decline of every aspect of her civilization except technology, the debasement of her arts, the cessation of novelty and progress, the complete disappearance of science after the second century, and the retreat from almost all that had spelled "the glory that was Greece, and the grandeur that was Rome." There are many indications that Greece had been smitten in the same way a few centuries earlier—when her genius suddenly declined and her population presently shrank—and that it was the importation of Greek wine-making and cookery into the Roman mansions which chiefly ruined the Roman aristocracy; but the proof for Greece is left for better Greek scholars. Here we present a completely new explanation for the Roman decay. . . .

A brief description is needed of this disease, unfamiliar to most of us although it is still the foremost industrial disease—and probably weakens all of us to some slight degree. It comes from lead or any of its compounds being taken in by mouth, lungs or perhaps the moist skin. With continued daily intake any dose greater than about one milligram a

* From *The Mankind Quarterly*, 5 (January–March 1965), 3–20. Reprinted by permission of author and publisher.

day may be dangerous, and a milligram is only 1/28,300th of an avoirdupois ounce. We are all getting about a quarter of that daily. Small amounts like these we can excrete, but any larger dosage is likely to pile up in the body, especially in the bones, whither it goes because of its kinship with calcium and where it does no observable harm. But when the store has become excessive, or when an acid condition of the body arises, perhaps through an alcoholic excess or an illness, then the lead is drawn out from the bones along with the calcium, and the person becomes evidently sick. But his symptoms are very varied and are unrelated to any particular act that might have enabled the Romans to perceive the connection with lead. Since the cause lay in the food and drink that all upper-class Romans consumed daily, how could they distinguish the morbific factor from everything else in their lives? Their physicians scarcely knew lead poisoning save as an acute accident or murder means, or perhaps as a disease of lead workers; and they had little to do with poor workers.

The varying symptoms of chronic plumbism include at first most conspicuously an obstinate and painful constipation, whose pain could be relieved by pressure around the navel and by opium —symptoms the Romans knew and recorded. Anemia, pallor, emaciation, a metallic taste in the mouth, dark stools, loss of appetite, and pains in the joints, are other signs. Further stages include paralysis of the extremities, starting with a peculiar wrist drop, headache, insomnia, blindness, and mental disturbances extending to insanity. "Crazy as a painter" was a proverb not long ago, when those craftsmen were usually lead poisoned. A wide range of further baleful effects occur in bad cases, including death. Those most interesting to us are various interferences with the fertility of men and especially of women, whom sufficient lead brings to sterility, miscarriage, stillbirth or premature labor; and their children born are apt to die prematurely.

Children also seem to be especially susceptible to plumbism, and the results are usually or perhaps always permanent physical or mental damage, such as epilepsy, if not death. Premature birth also often produces mental retardation. American city hospitals treat a succession of lead poisoned children, usually from the slums where they have developed *pica*, the habit of eating strange objects which include flecks of lead paint from old walls: lead is banned from modern interior paint. Also, infants crawl on the floor and then put their dusty hands in their mouths, whence, probably, the high death rate of children of lead-working fathers (Cantarow and Trumper 1944). The well-to-do Romans had lead paints, and the favorite color of their rich walls was the famous Pompeian red, colored by *minium*, a salt of lead or of mercury, also poisonous.

In summary, a markedly lead poisoned woman need expect no children at all to survive, and a moderately poisoned one would have few. Furthermore, if her husband were also hit hard by lead, perhaps sterile by it, or sick or dead, and if the family scattered table scraps and libations on the floor, as the Romans did, and some paint peeled off, then the *lares* and *penates* (which might also be leaden statuettes) would assuredly have no inheritor.

So who would take over the large and beautiful house, with its frescoed Pompeian red walls, and all the wealth, leadership and plutocratic power that went with it? Perhaps some nephew or cousin, further concentrating the wealth. But on the whole the missing wealthy must be replaced from below. Some able man born poor, perhaps the son of a freed slave, would scramble up the ladder, by luck, brains, energy and rapacity, gaining enough money to buy the house and secure the leadership functions. At first this might work pretty well, even if the able parvenu lacked the education, aristocratic traditions and prestige of the dying nobility. But when the same process had been repeated for generations, for six centuries as happened in Rome from the sack of Corinth until the pathetically named Romulus Augustulus shipped his nugatory crown to Constantinople, there would not remain much brains or beauty (or whatever qualities enable people to get money by one means or another) left in the lower classes, so persistently drained of their ablest, to replace the ever perishing rich and highly trained.

But were not the poor dying out at the same time, for the same reason? In Greece to some extent yes, but hardly in Rome. In both areas the poor were constantly reënforced in some degree by war-captured slaves, although the reproduction of these was much interfered with in various ways, especially the northern captives and other gang laborers in the Roman world. The diet of the poor was not so badly lead poisoned under the Romans. It is safe to say that the poor had not much wine, olive oil, grape sirup or drinks from other fruit or honey, or preserved fruits, these being the chief distinctive dietary sources of lead for the best people. Nor did they have the luxuries of cosmetics, nor so much lead paint around. They drank the same water which would be leaded if it came through lead pipes and was acid from decaying vegetation or from volcanic,

basaltic soil, or was neutral, like rainwater. Hard, alkaline water takes up no lead. But lead pipes were presumably less used in the country, where more of the poor and the unintellectual always live, than in the cities. The diet of the poor was mostly porridge, made from barley and other grains and perhaps acorns, but it also included bread, legumes and other vegetables, greens, vinegar, and a little meat, fish, milk, fresh or dried fruit, and wine. Less cooking might be done than for the rich since wood fuel was expensive, the nearby forest having been denuded, and transport being bad from lack of horseshoes and good harness. For cooking and liquid food storage the poor would be likely to use cheap earthenware, everywhere locally made, rather than expensive lead-lined bronze carried from afar, although this metal would save fuel. Where there were large groups of slaves the boiling and storing would be in larger pots than for the master's family, giving less leaded surface per unit of contents if the vessel were leaden or lead-plated. In any case it is perfectly clear from historical and epigraphic records that in the Roman Empire outside of Greece the poor, the mass, almost preserved their numbers, plagues notwithstanding, and the rich, having few children, did not. . . .

To understand further how lead could be ingested in so many ways by the ancient aristocracy, we should first explain its position among the metals and other substances that might have been substituted for it, especially as containers of acid food; for the relation of lead to the rest—its comparative merits as they seemed—was very different in ancient times from today.

Lead was a metal the ancients produced in superabundance, and hence used wholesale. It is the easiest of all metals (save sometimes iron) to mine, smelt and fashion, and needs only moderate heat. . . . Most of this dangerous metal they used in a great variety of domestic ways, often in contact with food or water, since they had so little idea of its poisonous nature. They used it for water pipes and containers, pots or their internal plating, cups, toys, statuettes, tokens, coins, lids, sieves, household repairs, solder, paint, cosmetics, external medicines, boxes, lead pencils, writing tablets, coffins and roofing. They alloyed it with copper (lead-bronze) and with tin (pewter), and used it in many other ways.

Lead was the only metal cheap enough for common use which they could join by welding, and the only one they could cast, save the rather expensive copper. Iron and steel they had in fair abundance but could shape only by hammering, punching, chiseling and grinding; they could not cast, weld, roll or draw iron or most other metals. Tin, which they were sometimes wise enough to use in food containers, was very expensive, twelve times the cost of its saturnine substitute. They were called by related names (*plumbum album et nigrum*), were doubtless sometimes confused, or the cheap one substituted by fraud, and the two were often alloyed. Silver was so precious as to be practically out of our purview. And those were all the metals they had, apart from gold, mercury and, in alloys, a little zinc, antimony, nickel, etc., none of which were significantly used with food.

Thus they could not cast a kettle of innocuous iron, or hammer out an iron skillet save with much difficulty. Their pottery, of common clay like our tiles, was weak, thick, porous and a poor conductor of heat. They naturally cast pots of copper or bronze when they could afford it. But then they easily learned well that when you leave acid food in any cuprous metal it produces verdigris, green and evident to the eye, bad to taste, and promptly bringing sickness. But lead produces none of these signals: its salts are light colored, tasteless or sweetish, and produce no immediate effects. In small doses lead, as we said, goes into the bones and stays there, harmless—until a considerable quantity is built up, which would usually have taken months or years. Instead of sickening you at once, like copper, it might kill your unborn child 20 years later; but you would never notice that connection. So, with fatal frequency, the well-to-do used leaden vessels, or lead-lined copper ones, for acid food, including most vegetables, especially for boiling. Heat greatly heightens chemical action, as we said. It was an easy matter to plate a bronze pot with lead or tin, or usually an alloy of the two; they simply heated the pot, then rubbed it on the inside with a piece of the low-melting metal. A cook could do it; and as one of the ancient writers said: "When the lead is worn off, renew it." That is, when you have eaten it up, eat some more. To be sure, they might use pure tin instead of lead for plating or for a solid cup, and they might use pottery or a glass or silver cup. But with fatal frequency, probably usually with heat, they used lead. The poor, on the other hand, with their different diet and pots, and their lack of other lead contacts, managed to survive and replace their masters. . . .

The proof of all these statements is not from the multiple, corroborating and unimpeachable ancient writings, in many more passages than cited herein, but from archeological finds of ancient lead equipment. If leaden objects rarely appear in museums it is because they rarely have high artistic value, and are a dull gray instead of the attractive green of corroded bronze. Furthermore, lead would be melted in fires like Pompeii's, and I think a thin lead or tin plating would have disappeared in 15 centuries underground.

From the skeletal remains of 22 people from the ancient world, Kobert and his student Rosenblatt (1906) found lead in the bones of two from Roman Carthage and two from the same city before the Roman conquest, including a child in a stone coffin—from which we can conclude it was of a rich family. The other 18 cases came from outside the Roman Empire, in time or place, and showed no lead, although five early ones showed tin, and one showed copper. The chemistry of 1906 hardly permitted more accuracy with bones than saying that a metal was detected or not. Later the dithizone and other methods have enabled much more sensitive and accurate analyses for lead. So in 1959 Specht and Fischer examined the remains of Pope Clement II, who had died nine centuries before and was buried in a stone coffin in Bamberg. They found so much lead in a rib that he must have died of plumbism. I have therefore set out to gather bones from the Roman Empire and from earlier Greece which can be identified from the conditions of burial as definitely rich or poor, and with further desirable data. My first samples are being analyzed by the Kettering Laboratory in the University of Cincinnati, which has been carrying out great and accurate studies of the occurrence of lead in bones today. Distinction will be made according to which bone is analyzed, since they store lead unequally, and also according to the subject's age and sex, and whether circulating ground waters would have deposited

lead therein, and how much. If it should appear that on the average the rich of the Imperial period were markedly poisoned by lead, and the poor not too much for reproduction, clinical research will have added a final seal of proof to evidence logically sufficient without it. Preliminary returns from my first 40 samples, analyzed by Dr. Robert A. Kehoe, are sufficiently consistent with the theory, but further analysis and more cases are needed, only seven so far being identifiably rich and 18 poor. . . .

One would also ask at once if other countries and ages have been similarly bedeviled by lead, besides Rome between 146 B.C. and 476 A.D. There is every indication, as we have often noted, that Greek genius had collapsed earlier still more suddenly, from the same pots and foods she had transmitted to Rome. Little Attica, which lit the world from Athens, may have laid the world low by her lead of Laurion. Egypt used lead in dangerous ways, such as in drinking tubes, and two or three times fell, after the Fifth, Twelfth and Eighteenth Dynasties, from progressive culture to near barbarism. What about Persia? When Alexander was slipping into alcoholism, insanity and death at 32, was he becoming lead poisoned? What about the Byzantines' lead glazes and their other artifacts?

When did western Europe learn to avoid eating lead? It must have been sometime in the Dark or Middle Ages. The first countries to show a revival of artistic ability, and interest in learning, were Ireland and Iceland. What did these two have in common, beside remoteness from Rome, and recent Christianization? A cool, rainy climate, entailing a pastoral economy and a milk diet —and milk is an antidote for lead.

M. I. ROSTOVTZEFF (1870–1952) was a phenomenally broad scholar whose range and productivity entitle him to be compared with Mommsen in the field of Roman history. He was forced to leave Russia after the Revolution and became a professor at the University of Wisconsin and later at Yale, where he trained some of today's leading ancient historians. In the selection below he reviews several economic explanations for the fall, including that of Huntington, and finds them inadequate in various ways.*

M. Rostovtzeff

The Decay of the Ancient World and Its Economic Explanations

Before I begin to deal with the economic theories of the decay of ancient civilization, let me define briefly what I mean by the Gibbonian term "decay" or "decline and fall." We are learning gradually that the term "decay" can hardly be applied to what happened in the ancient world in the time of the late Roman Empire and the beginning of the so-called Middle Ages. Historians do not now recognize that there was anything like "decay" of civilization in these periods. What happened was a slow and gradual change, a shifting of values in the consciousness of men. What seemed to be all-important to a Greek of the classical or Hellenistic period, or to an educated Roman of the time of the Republic and of the Early Empire, was no longer regarded as vital by the majority of men who lived in the late Roman Empire and the Early Middle Ages. They had their own notion of what was important, and most of what was essential in the classical period among the constituent parts of ancient civilization was discarded by them as futile and often detrimental. Since our point of view is more or less that of the classical peoples, we regard such an attitude of mind as a relapse into "barbarism," which in fact it is not. . . .

Thus to apply to events in the ancient world in the centuries after Diocletian

* From the *Economic History Review*, 2 (1929–1930), 197–214. Reprinted by permission of the Economic History Society.

and Constantine the term "decay" or "decline" is unfair and misleading. If, however, in the formula "decay of ancient civilization" we lay stress on "ancient" and not on "civilization," the formula hits the point. No doubt "ancient"—that is, "Greco-Roman"—civilization, the civilization of the world of Greco-Roman cities, of the Greek "politai" and Roman "cives,"* was gradually simplified, barbarized, reduced to its elements, and the bearers of this civilization, the cities and their inhabitants, gradually disappeared or changed their aspect almost completely. Cicero would not have recognized his compatriots if by chance he had come to life again in the Rome of the early popes and the late emperors, though some of them still wrote Ciceronian Latin. It is legitimate, therefore, to ask why did *ancient* civilization in its Greco-Roman form disappear. Since this disappearance chronologically coincides with the political disintegration of the Roman Empire and with a great change in its economic and social life, we may ask whether the whole set of phenomena described above is not in fact one phenomenon of which there is a single explanation.

It is not my intention to discuss here all the theories which have been suggested to explain the so-called decay of the ancient world. I have done it briefly in my *Social and Economic History of the Roman Empire*,† and I have no space in this short essay to repeat these statements in an enlarged form. The prevailing tendency among the historians of the ancient world and of the Middle Ages and among the economists is to look for one and the same explanation of all the phenomena mentioned above and to try to find one ultimate cause which would account for the many and various features of disintegration and decay which are typical of the times after Diocletian and Constantine, and which are usually comprised in the term "the decay of the ancient world." The most popular theory of this kind, a theory which was created by economists and has been accepted by some historians, is closely connected with the Marxian philosophy of history, the so-called economic materialism or "determinism," which became recently the official philosophy of history in Soviet Russia. We have this theory in many versions and modifications: one—less popular—is derived from many casual remarks of Marx himself; another, more popular among the historians though rejected by orthodox Marxists, was first formulated by Rodbertus, and was recently made a subject of vivid and somewhat violent discussion by K. Bücher and his opponents. It is useless to enumerate all the partial modifications of Bücher's theory, suggested by many prominent historians and economists, and still more useless is it to deal with the pure Marxian theory as formulated by Kautsky and others. Let me deal with Bücher and his scheme.

The scheme is well known and need not be repeated here. In my mind it is associated with the almost generally accepted theory of continuous and uninterrupted progress. Since antiquity stands at the beginning of known history, it must be primitive from the beginning to the end in all the fields of human evolution. Economically, therefore, it never reached, according to Bücher, a higher standard of development than

---

* *Politai* and *cives* are respectively the Greek and Latin words for "citizens"—Ed.

† See pp. 69–75.

that of house-economy. It was reserved for the Middle Ages to reach the next point—that of the city economy which led to the modern state-economy and to the beginning of world-economy. Since modern state-economy is closely connected with the development of capitalism in the modern world, Bücher himself and his followers insisted on the absence in the ancient world of any form of capitalism more or less similar to the capitalism of our modern times.

Bücher's theory, which he has quite recently defended with force and great learning in a violent debate with his chief opponents, E. Meyer and J. Beloch, is based chiefly on a careful investigation of two periods in the economic development of the ancient world: the fifth and fourth century B.C. in Athens, and the time of Diocletian. Since one of these periods lies at the beginning of the peculiar development of the Greek city-state, and the other represents the beginning of the disintegration of city life in the ancient world, the arguments of Bücher derived from the analysis of these two periods are far from convincing. We may say that Athens, in spite of an enormous progress in her economic life, was too near to the earlier stages of it not to show many and important features of house-economy, while the time of Diocletian, on the other hand, was the beginning of a new period in economic history resulting in an almost complete victory of house-economy, which came up again after a long period of latent existence in the form of survivals here and there in the early Roman Empire. Those forms of economic life which are most closely similar to the economic organization of modern times are characteristic, not of the early stages of ancient city-economy, as represented by

Athens of the fifth to the fourth century B.C., nor of the time of its decay in the period after Diocletian, but of the period of its blossom, the time between these two epochs—*i.e.,* the Hellenistic period on one hand and the early Roman Empire on the other. As long as the analysis of Bücher is confined to two sections only in the development of the ancient world, and is not extended to the Hellenistic and Roman periods, his arguments will not convince historians who are familiar with these two periods....

Bücher's theory does not stand alone among the endeavours to explain the so-called decay of the ancient world by economic causes. Quite recently two more suggestions have found a number of supporters among modern scholars, both historians and economists. One of these suggestions is not new. It was first formulated by Justus Liebig in a very general form. In the same general form it was repeated by Sigwart. Most of the ancient texts which bear out the suggestion have been collected and coordinated with the rest of our evidence by Salvioli. And finally, quite independently of his predecessors, Professor V. Simkhovitch came to the same idea and supported it by the same texts, being himself supported by T. Frank, F. F. Abbott, and A. C. Johnson. The formula is: the ancient world decayed because of the natural exhaustion of the soil in the area occupied by civilized man. The second theory is brand-new. It was first advanced by my colleague, Professor Ellsworth Huntington of Yale University, and the various aspects of it have been discussed by him and some other scholars in more than a score of books and articles in periodicals. Briefly stated, the theory suggests that climatic changes of a pulsatory character are largely responsible for both the impoverishment and the physical, moral and intellectual decay of the ancient world.

Let me deal first with the theory of exhaustion. In the first place, all the texts which speak of the exhaustion of the soil bear on Italy and to a certain extent on Greece, almost none (with some late exceptions) on the provinces of the Roman Empire. The set of texts which refer to Italy begins with the well-known pessimistic utterance of Lucretius (II. 1152 *ff*.), and ends with the equally well-known rhetorical utterances of the Fathers of the Christian Church. All these texts go back to the typical complaints of the farmers so familiar to everyone who had had to do with agriculturalists and agricultural life. Against them stands the description by Varro (*De re rust.* I. 2, 3, etc.) of Italy as the best cultivated and fertile land in the ancient world. The only scientific statement in this respect comes from the pen of Columella. The latter states that cornland in Italy gives in general very poor crops, and refers to complaints of farmers about the exhaustion of the soil in Italy. But Columella does not accept this explanation of the decay of agriculture in his time. He insists upon the fact that poor crops are the result, not of any exhaustion of the soil, but of poor agriculture; and he writes his textbook in order to show what ought to be done to restore Italy to her former agricultural prosperity. The statements about Greece are less explicit. None is of a scientific character. Almost all deal with the fact that there was in Greece a large amount of waste land, for whose cultivation there were no available human forces.

In the light of these statements have we the right to conclude that there was a general exhaustion of the soil throughout the Empire? The fact that since the end of the second century A.D. there was an increasing amount of waste land, both in Italy and in the provinces, does not necessarily mean that the soil was exhausted. I will return to this point later. And a careful analysis of our evidence, even as regards Italy and Greece, does not support the theory of exhaustion, even if applied to these two parts of the ancient world only.

In Italy we must sharply distinguish between two types of landowners or farmers. One was the old-fashioned peasant who depended entirely on his plot of land; the other was the modern farmer who invested his money in land exactly in the same way as he would invest it in a shop or house in the city or in a ship at sea. All the devices of systematic agriculture, as taught in the agricultural textbooks and manuals known in Greece and Rome, were applied to the second type of farm, but these textbooks were not extensively used by the majority of the peasants. Since the model farms were mostly in the hands of well-to-do or rich people, and there was in the first century B.C. and the first century A.D. a large demand for such farms, it is only natural that the best land was used for them, and the peasants were left with the poorer land all over Italy. The model farms concentrated not on grain, but on wine, oil, vegetables and fruit production. Land fit for pasture was used for cattle-breeding. No wonder, therefore, if grain-land in Italy—that is, peasant land—was gradually exhausted and yielded very poor crops. Poorly cultivated and neglected vineyards and olive groves would give equally poor crops. Complaints about the import of wine into Italy ought not to be taken seriously. Viticulture was flourishing there, not only in the time of Domitian (witness his famous measure which was the result of over-production of wine in Italy), but much later still. We should read the description of Herodian (VIII. 2, 3,) of the territory of Aquileia—a description which shows, by the way, that there was no exhaustion of soil and no waste land in the valley of the Po in his day. Nowadays the region of Aquileia is a vast marsh.

Thus exhaustion of the soil in Italy was a partial and secondary phenomenon in late Republican and early Imperial times. It was confined to a part of the land occupied by peasants and was typical only in some parts of the country. I am not referring here to the almost complete abandonment of some parts of South Italy and of the neighbourhood of Rome: this fact must be, and has been, ascribed to various causes which have very little to do with the exhaustion of the soil. What I am speaking of are the conditions of Central Italy, including, to a certain extent, Etruria. Later on the conditions changed. Slowly and gradually model-farming was given up and peasant-farming began to spread all over the country, invading even the estates of rich people. How far it contributed to the decay of agriculture and to the exhaustion of the soil we do not know; but it is certain that it was not caused by any exhaustion of the soil.

However it may be, even if Columella was wrong and Liebig and his followers are right as regards Italy, it is impossible to extend the same explanation to the provinces. We have not one text which supports it. Of course we know very little about the conditions of agriculture in the Roman provinces in the first two centuries A.D., yet we know enough to state that it throve in such lands as Gaul, Africa, Syria, and Asia Minor, not to speak of Egypt. And we have every reason to suppose that it was a paying concern in Macedonia, Thrace, and in the Danube provinces. One glance at the archæological evidence shows this with certainty; I mean the ruins of agricultural settlements, the so-called *villae,* spread far and wide over Britain, Gaul, Germany, Africa and Syria. In Africa and Syria large regions which were fertile and cultivated in ancient times are now waste and desolate.

And yet in the late third and in the following centuries we meet all over the Roman Empire large tracts of waste land which steadily increased in size and importance. Was this land abandoned because of the exhaustion of the soil? Exhaustion of the soil is a long and slow process; while the abandonment of land in the third and later centuries shows all the marks of a sudden catastrophe. The proof for believing that it was catastrophic is furnished by the history of Egypt. All the supporters of the theory of exhaustion point to Egypt as the only land where exhaustion was impossible. And so it is. Provided that the Nile does its duty, Egypt will yield abundant crops year after year. Nevertheless, Egypt shows the same phenomena as the rest of the Roman Empire in the third and the following centuries. All the borderlands of Egypt became waste and derelict: villages were abandoned: men were moving nearer to the Nile. Why? We know exactly the reason: misgovernment, excessive taxation, neglect of dikes and canals, discouragement of the population, lack of initiative.

If, therefore, there was exhaustion of

the soil in Italy and in the provinces in the centuries after the great crisis of the third century, this must be ascribed to man, not to nature. Men failed to support nature, though they knew as well as we do, or as the Japanese and the Chinese how it should be done. It is very probable that, in the late Roman Empire, exhaustion of the soil in some parts was a real calamity. But it was not this man-made calamity which caused the phenomena, even the economic phenomena, which we regard as typical of what is called the decay of the ancient world.

Huntington's theory is based on his climatological and geological observations. These observations, supported by some archæological evidence both in America and the Near East and by dendrological observations in California, led him to form a theory of climatic changes of a pulsatory character in the historical period. These changes do not affect temperature very much. In this respect climate has remained fairly uniform in historical times. They very greatly affect, however, the relative storminess of a given area, and cause rapid and sudden decreases and increases in rainfall and in general moisture. Such changes are of great importance, according to Huntington, for the development of civilization. They affect the fertility of the soil, create marshland and therefore malaria, and influence the conditions of health, the mood and character, the activity and working power of the population. Thus decline of civilization ought to coincide with periods of dryness, brilliant development of it with periods of moisture. At least *ceteris paribus* civilization cannot thrive in regions with a climate too cold or too warm, too moist or too dry. I have no means of checking the re-

sults arrived at by Huntington as regards the pulsations of climate. His observations on the trees and lakes of California are very convincing. Less so are his archæological observations especially in Syria: they must be checked by specialists. On the ground of these observations Huntington drew up two diagrams: one showing the pulsations of climate in the Near East, another showing the same pulsations, that is the increase and decrease of moisture and storminess, in California. In a very general way the two coincide. These diagrams he has used for explaining the history of Rome as one of his historical illustrations. Though he has no special diagram for Southern Europe and no observations on trees, lakes and ruins in Italy, he regards the Californian diagram as applicable to Italy, since nowadays its climate, particularly that of Rome and Naples, is almost identical with that of California.

In my opinion, though I state it with regret, this theory, whether true or not in itself, does not help the historians of the ancient world as far as Rome is concerned. According to Huntington, the period 450–250 B.C. was a period of abundant rains and good climate in Rome. Hence, he concludes, Rome laid the foundations of her strength. A change occurred at about 220–210 and lasted until about 121 B.C. Huntington, quoting Ferrero, calls this a time of great moral and economic changes, of catastrophical decay. How about the second Punic War, the conquest of the Orient, and the creation of the Roman Empire? Are they also signs of decay and dryness? From 121 B.C. to 20 A.D. he finds a great improvement; yet this was the time of the Gracchi and of the agrarian laws, and the time also of the great political and social revolution which lasted for more than half of the blessed period of moisture. Or are the revolutions caused by increase in moisture and by more invigorating air? From 20 to 180 A.D. there is said to have been another great period of dryness, which partly coincides with the greatest period of the Roman Empire, and a rise in moisture about 180–200 A.D. sloping slowly down until 300 A.D. Again the largest part of this period of improvement in climate is occupied by the prolonged civil war of the third century. Then there was a great fall in moisture in the fourth century, which was a time of temporary improvement in the economic conditions of the Roman Empire.

I am afraid the diagram of Californian conditions either does not apply to Italy and needs alteration, or else the pulsatory changes of climate have affected the development of the Roman State very little. At least I am unable to find any relation between Huntington's diagram and the events of Roman History.

But suppose that the theory of climatic pulsations is correct. Have the pulsations such an enormous importance for the development of human civilization? They may cause some catastrophic phenomena, especially in the desert. It is not impossible that some of the great migrations of the Asiatic nomads were caused by pulsatory changes in climate. And we may suppose that the periodical drives of nomads in the so-called "fertile crescent" in the Near East may have been connected with a set of dry years. Such changes, however, can hardly have had great importance in lands like Italy and the rest of Europe. Civilized men, with the help of a well-developed technique, can easily combat the bad effects of periods of dryness. Witness the two lands which Huntington has studied closely: Palestine and Italy. They both live now in a period of acute dryness, and yet in both the last years have been years of great economic, and especially of agricultural, revival. And it is to be noted that in Italy the work of revival has been carried out mostly in the neighbourhood of Rome and in the South, not in the North.

ROSTOVTZEFF'S most widely read book is his *Social and Economic History of the Roman Empire* (1926), from which the concluding passage is reprinted below. In it he attributes the breakdown of the Empire to an unfortunate transformation of its social structure. A common criticism of this theory is that it was probably suggested to him by his own tragic experience at having to leave Russia at the time of the Revolution. The rhetorical questions with which the book concludes perhaps suggest that Rostovtzeff had not definitely formulated his own thesis.*

M. Rostovtzeff

The Oriental Despotism

Every reader of a volume devoted to the Roman Empire will expect the author to express his opinion on what is generally, since Gibbon, called the decline and fall of the Roman Empire, or rather of ancient civilization in general. I shall therefore briefly state my own view on this problem, after defining what I take the problem to be. The decline and fall of the Roman Empire, that is to say, of ancient civilization as a whole, has two aspects: the political, social, and economic on the one hand, and the intellectual and spiritual on the other. In the sphere of politics we witness a gradual barbarization of the Empire from within, especially in the West. The foreign, German, elements play the leading part both in the government and in the army, and settling in masses displace the Roman population, which disappears from the fields. A related phenomenon, which indeed was a necessary consequence of this barbarization from within, was the gradual disintegration of the Western Roman Empire; the ruling classes in the former Roman provinces were replaced first by Germans and Sarmatians, and later by Germans alone, either through peaceful penetration or by conquest. In the East we observe a gradual orientalization of the Byzantine Empire, which leads ultimately to the establishment, on the ruins of the Roman Empire, of strong half-oriental and purely oriental states, the

* From M. Rostovtzeff, *The Social and Economic History of the Roman Empire* (2d ed.; Oxford, 1957), vol. I, 523–541. Reprinted by permission of the Clarendon Press, Oxford.

Caliphate of Arabia, and the Persian and Turkish empires. From the social and economic point of view, we mean by decline the gradual relapse of the ancient world to very primitive forms of economic life, into an almost pure "house-economy." The cities, which had created and sustained the higher forms of economic life, gradually decayed, and the majority of them practically disappeared from the face of the earth. A few, especially those that had been great centres of commerce and industry, still lingered on. The complicated and refined social system of the ancient Empire follows the same downward path and becomes reduced to its primitive elements: the king, his court and retinue, the big feudal landowners, the clergy, the mass of rural serfs, and small groups of artisans and merchants. Such is the political, social, and economic aspect of the problem. However, we must not generalize too much. The Byzantine Empire cannot be put on a level with the states of Western Europe or with the new Slavonic formations. But one thing is certain: on the ruins of the uniform economic life of the cities there began everywhere a special, locally differentiated, evolution.

From the intellectual and spiritual point of view the main phenomenon is the decline of ancient civilization, of the city civilization of the Greco-Roman world. The Oriental civilizations were more stable: blended with some elements of the Greek city civilization, they persisted and even witnessed a brilliant revival in the Caliphate of Arabia and in Persia, not to speak of India and China. Here again there are two aspects of the evolution. The first is the exhaustion of the creative forces of Greek civilization in the domains where its great triumphs had been achieved, in the exact sciences,

in technique, in literature and art. The decline began as early as the second century B.C. There followed a temporary revival of creative forces in the cities of Italy, and later in those of the Eastern and Western provinces of the Empire. The progressive movement stopped almost completely in the second century A.D. and, after a period of stagnation, a steady and rapid decline set in again. Parallel to it, we notice a progressive weakening of the assimilative forces of Greco-Roman civilization. The cities no longer absorb—that is to say, no longer hellenize or romanize—the masses of the country population. The reverse is the case. The barbarism of the country begins to engulf the city population. Only small islands of civilized life are left, the senatorial aristocracy of the late Empire and the clergy; but both, save for a section of the clergy, are gradually swallowed up by the advancing tide of barbarism.

Another aspect of the same phenomenon is the development of a new mentality among the masses of the population. It was the mentality of the lower classes, based exclusively on religion and not only indifferent but hostile to the intellectual achievements of the higher classes. This new attitude of mind gradually dominated the upper classes, or at least the larger part of them. It is revealed by the spread among them of the various mystic religions, partly Oriental, partly Greek. The climax was reached in the triumph of Christianity. In this field the creative power of the ancient world was still alive, as is shown by such momentous achievements as the creation of the Christian church, the adaptation of Christian theology to the mental level of the higher classes, the creation of a powerful Christian literature and of a new Christian art. The new intellectual efforts aimed chiefly at influencing the mass of the population and therefore represented a lowering of the high standards of city-civilization, at least from the point of view of literary forms.

We may say, then, that there is one prominent feature in the development of the ancient world during the imperial age, alike in the political, social, and economic and in the intellectual field. It is a gradual absorption of the higher classes by the lower, accompanied by a gradual levelling down of standards. This levelling was accomplished in many ways. There was a slow penetration of the lower classes into the higher, which were unable to assimilate the new elements. There were violent outbreaks of civil strife: the lead was taken by the Greek cities, and there followed the civil war of the first century B.C. which involved the whole civilized world. In these struggles the upper classes and the city-civilization remained victorious on the whole. Two centuries later, a new outbreak of civil war ended in the victory of the lower classes and dealt a mortal blow to the Greco-Roman civilization of the cities. Finally, that civilization was completely engulfed by the inflow of barbarous elements from outside, partly by penetration, partly by conquest, and in its dying condition it was unable to assimilate even a small part of them.

The main problem, therefore, which we have to solve is this. Why was the city civilization of Greece and Italy unable to assimilate the masses, why did it remain a civilization of the *élite*, why was it incapable of creating conditions which should secure for the ancient world a continuous, uninterrupted movement along the same path of urban civilization? In other words: why had modern civilization to be built up laboriously as something new on the ruins of the old, instead of being a direct continuation of it? Various explanations have been suggested, and each of them claims to have finally solved the problem. Let us then review the most important of them. They may be divided into four classes.

(1) The political solution is advocated by many distinguished scholars. For Beloch the decay of ancient civilization was caused by the absorption of the Greek city-states by the Roman Empire, by the formation of a world-state which prevented the creative forces of Greece from developing and consolidating the great achievements of civilized life. There is some truth in this view. It is evident that the creation of the Roman Empire was a step forward in the process of levelling, and that it facilitated the final absorption of the higher classes. We must, however, take into consideration that class war was a common feature of Greek life, and that we have not the least justification for supposing that the Greek city-community would have found a solution of the social and economic problems which produced civil war in the various communities. Further, this view suggests that there was only one creative race in the ancient world, which is notoriously false. Another explanation, tending in the same direction, has been put forward by Kornemann. He regards as the main cause of the decay of the Roman Empire the fact that Augustus reduced the armed forces of the Empire, and that this reduction was maintained by his successors. The suggestion lays the whole emphasis on the military side of the problem, and is therefore a return to the antiquated idea that ancient civilization was destroyed by the barbarian invasions, an idea which should not be resuscitated. Be-

sides, the maintenance of a comparatively small army was imperatively imposed by the economic weakness of the Empire, a fact which was understood by all the emperors. Still less convincing is the idea of Ferrero, that the collapse of the Empire was due to a disastrous event, to an accident which had the gravest consequences. He holds that by transmitting his power to his son Commodus instead of to a man chosen by the senate, M. Aurelius undermined the senate's authority on which the whole fabric of the Roman state rested; that the murder of Commodus led to the usurpation of Septimius and to the civil war of the third century; and that the usurpation and the war destroyed the authority of the senate and deprived the imperial power of its only legitimacy in the eyes of the population which was its main support. Ferrero forgets that legally the power of the emperors in the third century was still derived from the senate and people of Rome, that it was so even in the time of Diocletian, and that the same idea still survived under Constantine and his successors. He also forgets that the subtle formula of Augustus, Vespasian, and the Antonines was incomprehensible to the mass of the people of the Empire, and was a creation of the upper classes, completely outside the range of popular conceptions. Finally, he fails to understand the true character of the crisis of the third century. The struggle was not between the senate and the emperor, but between the cities and the army—that is to say, the masses of peasants—as is shown by the fact that the lead in the fight was taken not by Rome but by the cities of the province of Africa. A deeper explanation is offered by Heitland. He suggests that the ancient world decayed because it was unable to give the masses

a share in the government, and even gradually restricted the numbers of those who participated in the life of the state, ultimately reducing them to the emperor himself, his court, and the imperial bureaucracy. I regard this point as only one aspect of the great phenomenon which I have described above. Have we the right to suppose that the emperors would not have tried the plan of representative government if they had known of it and believed in it? They tried many other plans and failed. If the idea of representative government was foreign to the ancient world (and as a matter of fact it was not), why did the ancient world not evolve the idea, which is not a very difficult one? Moreover, the question arises, Can we be sure that representative government is the cause of the brilliant development of our civilization and not one of its aspects, just as was the Greek city-state? Have we the slightest reason to believe that modern democracy is a guarantee of continuous and uninterrupted progress, and is capable of preventing civil war from breaking out under the fostering influence of hatred and envy? . . .

(2) The economic explanation of the decay of the ancient world must be rejected completely. In speaking of the development of industry in the ancient world, I have dealt with the theory of K. Bücher, accepted with modifications by M. Weber and G. Salvioli. If the theory fails to explain even this minor point, much less will it serve to explain the general phenomenon. Those who defend this theory forget that the ancient world went through many cycles of evolution, and that in these cycles there occur long periods of progress and other long periods of return to more primitive conditions, to the phase of economic life which is generally described as "house-

economy." It is true that the ancient world never reached the economic stage in which we live. But in the history of the ancient world we have many epochs of high economic development: certain periods in the history of many Oriental monarchies, particularly Egypt, Babylonia, and Persia; the age of the highest development of the city-states, especially the fourth century B.C.; the period of the Hellenistic monarchies, where the climax was reached in the third century B.C.; the period of the late Roman Republic and of the early Roman Empire. All these periods show different aspects of economic life and different aspects of capitalism. In none of them did the forms of house-economy pervail. We may compare the economic aspect of life during these periods to that of many European countries in the time of the Renaissance and later, although in no case would the comparison be perfect, as there is no identity between the economic development of the modern and that of the ancient world. According to the different economic conditions of these several periods in the history of the ancient world, the relations between house-economy and capitalistic economy varied, and they frequently varied not only in the different periods but also in different parts of the ancient world during the same period. The ancient world was in this respect not unlike the modern world. In the industrial countries of Europe, such as England and some parts of Germany and France, economic life nowadays is by no means the same as it is in the agricultural countries, like Russia and the Balkan peninsula and large parts of the Near East. The economic life of the United States of America is not in the least identical with the economic life of Europe or of the various parts of South America, not

to speak of China, Japan, and India. So it was in the ancient world. While Egypt and Babylonia had a complex economic life, with a highly developed industry and wide commercial relations, other parts of the Near East lived a quite different and much more primitive life. While Athens, Corinth, Rhodes, Syracuse, Tyre, and Sidon in the fourth century B.C. were centres of a developed commercial capitalism, other Greek cities lived an almost purely agricultural life. In the Hellenistic and Roman periods it was just the same. The main fact which has to be explained is why capitalistic development, which started at many times and in many places, and prevailed in large portions of the ancient world for comparatively long periods, yielded ultimately to more primitive forms of economic life. Even in our own times it has not completely ousted those forms. It is evident that the problem cannot be solved by affirming that the ancient world lived throughout under the forms of primitive house-economy. The statement is manifestly wrong. We might say exactly the same of large areas of the modern world, and we are not at all sure that a violent catastrophe might not bring the modern capitalistic world back to the primitive phase of house-economy.

To sum up what I have said, the economic simplification of ancient life was not the cause of what we call the decline of the ancient world, but one of the aspects of the more general phenomenon which the theories mentioned above try to explain. Here, just as in the other spheres of human life, the political, social, intellectual, and religious, the more primitive forms of life among the masses were not absorbed by the higher forms but triumphed over them in the end. We may select one of these phenomena and declare it to be the ultimate cause; but it would be an arbitrary assumption which would not convince any one. The problem remains. Why was the victorious advance of capitalism stopped? Why was machinery not invented? Why were the business systems not perfected? Why were the primal forces of primitive economy not overcome? They were gradually disappearing; why did they not disappear completely? To say that they were quantitatively stronger than in our own times does not help us to explain the main phenomenon. That is why many economists, who are aware that the usual explanation only touches the surface and does not probe the problem to the bottom, endeavour to save the economic explanation, and the materialistic conception of historical evolution in general, by producing some potent physical factor as the cause of the weakness of the higher forms of economic life in the ancient world. Such a factor has been found by some scholars in the general exhaustion of the soil all over the ancient world, which reached its climax in the late Roman Empire and ruined the ancient world.... There are no facts to support it. All the facts about the economic development of the ancient world speak against it. Agriculture decayed in the ancient world just in the same way and from the same causes as the other branches of economic life. As soon as the political and social conditions improved in the various parts of the Empire, the fields and gardens began to yield the same harvests as before. Witness the flourishing state of Gaul in the time of Ausonius and of Sidonius Apollinaris; witness the fact that in Egypt, where the soil is inexhaustible and those parts of it which are not flooded are very easily improved by the most primitive methods, **agriculture decayed in the**

third and fourth centuries, just as in the other provinces. It is plain that the economic explanation does not help us, and that the investigations of the economists reveal, not the cause of the decline of the ancient world, but merely one of its aspects.

(3) The rapid progress of medicine and of biological science has had its influence on the problem of the decay of ancient civilization. A biological solution has been often suggested, and the theories of degeneration and race-suicide have been applied to the ancient world. The biological theory supplies us with an apparently exhaustive explanation of the decline of the assimilative forces of the civilized upper classes. They gradually degenerated and had not the power to assimilate the lower classes but were absorbed by them. According to Seeck, the cause of their degeneration and of their numerical decline was the "extermination of the best" by foreign and civil wars. Others, like Tenney Frank, think of the contamination of higher races by an admixture of the blood of inferior races. Others, again, regard degeneration as a natural process common to all civilized communities: the best are neither exterminated nor contaminated, but they commit systematic suicide by not reproducing and by letting the inferior type of mankind breed freely. I am not competent to sit in judgement on the problem of degeneration from the biological and physiological point of view. From the historical point of view, I venture to remark against Seeck that in wars and revolutions it is not only the best that are exterminated. On the other hand, revolutions do not always prevent the succeeding period from being a period of great bloom. Against Frank I may suggest that I see no criterion for distinguishing between inferior and

superior races. Why are the Greek and Latin races considered the only superior races in the Roman Empire? Some of the races which "contaminated" the ruling races, for instance, the pre-Indo-European and pre-Semitic race or races of the Mediterranean, had created great civilizations in the past (the Egyptian, the Minoan, the Iberian, the Etruscan, the civilizations of Asia Minor), and the same is true of the Semitic and of the Iranian civilizations. Why did the admixture of the blood of these races contaminate and deteriorate the blood of the Greeks and the Romans? On the other hand, the Celts and the Germans belonged to the same stock as the Greeks and the Romans. The Celts had a high material civilization of their own. The Germans were destined to develop a high civilized life in the future. Why did the admixture of their blood corrupt and not regenerate their fellow Aryans, the Greeks and the Romans? The theory of a natural decay of civilization by race-suicide states the same general phenomenon of which we have been speaking, the gradual absorption of the upper classes by the lower and the lack of assimilative power shown by the upper. It states the fact, but gives no explanation. The problem this theory has to solve is, Why do the best not reproduce their kind? It may be solved in different ways: we may suggest an economic, or a physiological, or a psychological explanation. But none of these explanations is convincing.

(4) Christianity is very often made responsible for the decay of ancient civilization. This is, of course, a very narrow point of view. Christianity is but one side of the general change in the mentality of the ancient world. Can we say that this change is the ultimate cause of the decay of ancient civilization? It is not easy to discriminate between causes and symptoms, and one of the urgent tasks in the field of ancient history is a further investigation of this change of mentality. The change, no doubt, was one of the most potent factors in the gradual decay of the civilization of the city-state and in the rise of a new conception of the world and of a new civilization. But how are we to explain the change? Is it a problem of individual and mass psychology?

None of the existing theories fully explains ... the decay of ancient civilization, if we can apply the word "decay" to the complex phenomenon which I have endeavoured to describe. Each of them, however, has contributed much to the clearing of the ground, and has helped us to perceive that the main phenomenon which underlies the process of decline is the gradual absorption of the educated classes by the masses and the consequent simplification of all the functions of political, social, economic, and intellectual life, which we call the barbarization of the ancient world.

The evolution of the ancient world has a lesson and a warning for us. Our civilization will not last unless it be a civilization not of one class, but of the masses. The Oriental civilizations were more stable and lasting than the Greco-Roman, because, being chiefly based on religion, they were nearer to the masses. They have destroyed the upper classes, and resulted in accelerating the process of barbarization. But the ultimate problem remains like a ghost, ever present and unlaid: Is it possible to extend a higher civilization to the lower classes without debasing its standard and diluting its quality to the vanishing point? Is not every civilization bound to decay as soon as it begins to penetrate the masses?

MEYER REINHOLD* (1909–   ), Professor of
Classical Studies at the University of Missouri, published this critique of Rostovtzeff two decades after the
Social and Economic History appeared. In it he
sharply emphasizes the dangers of modernization and
questions whether we should really use modern
terminology in speaking of "classes" in antiquity. He
also asks to what degree "capitalism" in the modern
sense really existed under the Empire.*

Meyer Reinhold

Historian of the Classic World:
A Critique of Rostovtzeff

The fundamental doctrine of Rostovtzeff's historical "intuition" is the view
that "... the ancient world experienced,
on a smaller scale, the same process of
development which we are experiencing
now.... The modern development...
differs from the ancient only in quantity
and not in quality." This basic axiom of
the absence of qualitative differences between the structure of ancient civilization and that of modern capitalist society
permits a transposition to antiquity of
the pattern and categories of the capitalist mode of production and exchange,
its class structure, ideological configura-
tions, and special terminology. All of
Rostovtzeff's major efforts in the field
of social and economic history are "mod-
ernized" with such concepts as "capitalists," "bourgeoisie," "proletariat," "factories," and "mass production."

True, under pressure of criticism and
of the objective facts themselves, he
retreated to a more moderate position.
He conceded that the similarities between ancient and modern economy are
superficial, that "the general trend is
utterly different." Nevertheless, he has
continued to believe in a "peculiar" form
of capitalism, an "infant capitalistic system," "more or less similar to modern
capitalism," whose most highly developed stage "... may be compared, to a
certain extent, with the development of
modern Europe in the seventeenth, eighteenth, and early nineteenth centuries.

* From *Science and Society*, 10 (1946), 361–391. Reprinted by permission of Science
and Society, Inc.

And yet it is so utterly different." His latest formulation is that "The innovations in the organization of economic life . . . tended towards what, with all reserve, we may call 'capitalism' (I hesitate to use a term whose meaning is so much disputed) . . ."

. . . That some attributes of the capitalist system of production were present with varying degrees of intensity in certain periods of antiquity is not to be denied. Rostovtzeff's definition of "ancient capitalism" confounds the part with the whole. For it is certain that some of the factors detailed by him were either not to be found in or were peripheral to the economic order of the ancient world, and that he ignores some of the decisive characteristics of capitalism, for example, the primacy of the wage system and the profit motive, long-term planning and a scientific system of capital accounting, and an expanding market. Finally, the earliest form of capitalism emerging at the twilight of the feudal epoch can be shown to be qualitatively different from all analogous manifestations in antiquity.

It is apparent that Rostovtzeff has often used the term "capitalism" in a much looser fashion. Mere bigness, abstractly conceived without reference to the mode of production, is at times associated in his thinking with the nature of capitalism. Equating capital with precious metals, money, and wealth, in an economically naive fashion, he regards such magnates as the wealthy Roman senators of the first century B.C., in whose hands were concentrated large amounts of landed property, as "great capitalists." Further, he regards "capitalistic agriculture" both in Greece and in Italy as developing from the absorption of small peasant holdings into large landed estates. Moreover, since he is aware that the primacy of commerce and industry over agriculture is a precondition for the proper functioning of capitalism, the mere existence of relatively intense commercial and industrial enterprise in a society (as, for example, Athens, the Hellenistic world, and the early Roman Empire) is sufficient ground for classifying its economy as "capitalistic," even though, as he is well aware, these activities were not the prevailing and decisive ones in the economic life but secondary and peripheral to agriculture.

Here the economic prejudices of Rostovtzeff run counter to the objective facts, scientifically established by himself, which reveal unmistakably that the foundation of economic life in all periods of antiquity for all classes was agriculture, upon which rested the ancillary superstructure of commerce and industry. Yet, under the sway of his original preconception, he is convinced, intuitively, that the main source of wealth in the Hellenistic world and in the early Roman Empire was commercial enterprise, which, together with a flourishing industry, pumped capital into the land and introduced the methods of "scientific agriculture." The well-known facts that agriculture was the predominant form of economic life, that only a small fraction of the wealth of the ancient world was invested in commerce and industry, and that the major part of income derived by the wealthy from all sources was expended by them upon luxury consumption, enlargement of landed holdings, unproductive private and public building construction, and warfare— facts which Rostovtzeff not only recognizes but demonstrates—preclude the possibility that ancient society was at any period of its development capital-istic in nature. For under capitalism the relationship between productive rein-vestment of profits and unproductive expenditure is reversed. The unproduc-tive consumption of wealth, character-istic of societies in which landed wealth is primary, acts as a fetter arresting the development of productive forces.

Rostovtzeff admits that handicraft pro-duction in the home or by individual artisans in small workshops for a re-stricted local market, at the order of the consumer, was the predominant form of industry. He is, moreover, convinced that "commercial capitalism" "... which started at many times and in many places, and prevailed in large portions of the ancient world for comparatively long periods ... never reached the eco-nomic stage in which we live, the stage of industrial capitalism," but he pro-fesses to see in the industrial evolution of antiquity the earliest known tendency toward mass production of standardized goods for an indefinite market. That this is a subjective view which does not accord with the known evidence is, in fact, finally conceded by Rostovtzeff. Yet, he describes Greek industry in the fifth and fourth centuries B.C. as "modern-ized" and developing along "capitalistic" lines. And though he has modified earlier views about the existence of "large factories" and "great industrial firms," he still clings to the belief, unsupported by the sources, that antiquity developed "specialized shops, approaching in char-acter to small factories," "factories," "larger factory-like undertakings," "es-tablishments resembling factories." This despite his full realization that mecha-nization was almost completely absent, that technological progress in industry was not radical and dynamic but actually

of negligible importance (except in mili-tary engineering and building construc-tion), that, in fact, during the Roman Empire there was a noticeable decline in technique. And he is full aware of the fact that "The fabric of Roman in-dustry rested ... on very weak founda-tions, and on such foundations no capitalist industry could be built up," because the purchasing power of the great masses of the population through-out antiquity was too low "... to acquire anything whatever outside the limits of their most urgent needs." "Hence in-dustry is carried on to supply the needs of a comparatively small number...."

The primitive methods, costliness, in-security and slowness of all types of transport in antiquity are abundantly clear to Rostovtzeff. But he proceeds from a preconceived notion of a "nat-ural" centralized system of production, and accordingly views the predominantly local character of ancient manufacture, imposed by the fetters of transportation limitations, as a calculated deviation from such a "natural" centralization. For the restricted range of industrial output and the absence of great industrial centers are attributed by Rostovtzeff, in one of his pet theories, to political or economic policies (in both the Hellenis-tic states and in the Roman Empire) of local self-sufficiency and emancipation from foreign markets. Trade in the prime necessities of life (especially grain) to supply the requirements of the mili-tary and of administrative and urban centers, and traffic in slaves and luxury articles for the few, admittedly consti-tuted the main lines of commercial enter-prise. This trade barely touched the surface of the basic structure of ancient economy: it did not penetrate every phase of economic life nor transform large areas into economically interdependent complexes. Such a development is not possible without modern techniques of transportation and communication. Yet Rostovtzeff has projected into antiquity the essentially modern concept of "economic unity" of extensive areas, even of entire civilizations.

The same objections must be raised against the concepts "scientific agriculture" and "capitalistic farming" employed by Rostovtzeff. It is clear that he understands by these terms merely large-scale agriculture. To his thinking, peasant economy and tenant farming by small holders preclude scientific management and advanced agricultural technique, which require abundant capital. Here again he is projecting modern conditions into antiquity. For it has been demonstrated by Mickwitz that scientific, rationalized agriculture is a product of modern times, very different from the empirical farm management and agricultural technique of the ancient world.

It is not surprising, therefore, that, glossing over the impoverishment of the masses by an economic system which enriched a small propertied minority, Rostovtzeff should define "prosperity" subjectively in terms of the well-being of a commercial and business class. "I use the term 'prosperity,'" he says, "to describe the general conditions of a period: progress in production, brisk trade, accumulation of capital. General prosperity did not necessarily mean that the working classes enjoyed tolerably satisfactory conditions. They were the last to profit by it." The image conjured up in his mind by the word "prosperity" is the existence of a strong urban bourgeoisie, a moderately well-to-do "middle class," possessing sizeable sums of money. The

subjectivity of this formulation is evidenced by the fact that the wealth of kings, extensive building operations both public and private, and idle accumulations of hoarded wealth are often regarded by him as signs of prosperity. It is clear that the standard of living and purchasing power of the masses of the population of a society do not figure in Rostovtzeff's conception of "prosperity"—even though the working masses should constitute for him the "economic backbone" of that society. The term "proletariat," employed by him without clear reference to the prevalent mode of production as a very loose label for all but the propertied minority, is a catch-all for "free wage earners and slaves," "paupers," "the mob," "rabble of the citizens," "working class," "have-nots," "poor peasants," "lower classes," "unemployed men in the cities, tenants and hired laborers in the country."

These judgments and values of Rostovtzeff reveal a pattern of social ideology which probably took form during the turbulent transition from tsarism to the Soviet regime in the land of his birth. His understanding of the term "bourgeoisie" must also be placed in the context of pre-Soviet Russian society, predominantly agricultural, under the sway of a decaying feudal landed aristocracy, emerging into the dawn of industrial capitalism, and generating an enterprising bourgeoisie and a growing industrial proletariat. Situated socially and economically in an intermediate position between the declining but politically dominant ruling nobility and the increasingly class-conscious peasants and industrial workers, the Russian bourgeoisie was truly a *middle class*, drawing its income both from commercial and industrial enterprise and from rationalized agriculture. But it never succeeded, as did its counterparts in the more advanced capitalist countries, in becoming a ruling class. In the developed capitalist countries the polarization of classes into a big bourgeoisie and a proletariat left a heterogeneous "... aggregation of functional groups wavering between the proletariat and the bourgeoisie...," often called the petty-bourgeoisie or "middle class." It is methodologically important to distinguish between the bourgeois middle class of early capitalism and the petty-bourgeois "middle class" of developed capitalism, which is not a true economic class.

This confusion of a bourgeoisie as a ruling class and as a "middle class" is evident in Rostovtzeff's economic and social writings. It is true that he has attempted to give precise definition to the concept "bourgeoisie" in economic terms:

> I understand by it ... a class of men who had achieved by their efforts or inherited from their parents a certain degree of prosperity, and lived not on the income derived by manual labour but from the investment of their accumulated capital in some branch of economic activity.... The main and most characteristic feature of the *bourgeoisie* from an economic standpoint was ... the fact that they were no professionals, craftsmen of one kind or another, salaried employees, or the like, but investors of accumulated capital and employers of labour.

The bourgeois is the "average citizen," "... not an aristocrat by birth and wealth.... He is a middle-class landowner, a business man, or a *rentier*, well-to-do but not extremely rich." A careful study of his application interchangeably of the terms "bourgeoisie" and "middle class" to ancient times reveals that they serve to distinguish in his mind, a moderately well-to-do propertied urban class from a fabulously wealthy minority and from the less prosperous or propertyless masses.

The income of this class may be derived from investments in agriculture, trade, or industry. At times they may be very rich men, or even, constituting a petty-bourgeoisie, shopowners, moneychangers, artisans, members of the liberal professions. It is even possible for members of this "middle class" to be poor. But his scientific reading of the evidence also forces him to document the decisive conclusion that the class which he has subjectively moulded into a "bourgeois middle class" is actually the *ruling class* both of the Hellenistic states and of the Roman Empire, whose economic interests were centered exclusively or predominantly in landowning! His "bourgeois middle class" is a myth.

An important source of these confusions in Rostovtzeff's thinking is his failure to clarify the relation of his "bourgeoisie" to the machinery of state power both in Hellenistic and Roman imperial times. In general this class is treated as separated from the state and its policies. It is, therefore, not regarded as responsible for economic disasters. On the contrary, it is viewed as the principal sufferer from such catastrophes, and the responsibility for them is sought outside this class, which is pictured as squeezed between the pressure of the state from above and the masses from below. The threat of proletarianization by the big bourgeoisie and the threat of expropriation by the proletariat; opposition "... downward against the political and social demands of the laboring classes ... and upward against monopoly capital"— leading traits of the modern petty-bourgeois ideology—are a mainspring of Rostovtzeff's subjective interpretation of the data of antiquity. Idealizing a capitalist society which nourishes a large and prosperous urban "middle class," and yearning for stability in the social and economic order, he views with apprehension economic bigness, concentration of wealth in the hands of the few, which brings in its train large masses of poor. For economic crises and social disorders are then inevitable, and since he regards the masses as incapable of ruling, tyranny and economic enslavement may follow. Hence, wherever in the history of mankind there is "prosperity" as he understands it, Rostovtzeff assumes a priori the existence of a "bourgeois" class.

This class is idealized by Rostovtzeff, in his social studies of the ancient world, as peaceful, thrifty, industrious, ". . . the most civilized and best educated classes of the urbanized parts of the [Roman] Empire." While admitting grave faults in the Hellenistic "bourgeoisie," he emphasizes its sturdy character and its preservation of the leading traits of Greek city life for posterity. "In my opinion it was the city *bourgeoisie* that was chiefly responsible for the great struggle for liberty carried on by the cities [of the Hellenistic world] . . . ," though he acknowledges that ". . . the *bourgeoisie* was often prepared to make far-reaching concessions to the kings, especially when faced with social revolution from within." It constitutes for him the leading force of the Hellenistic world and the Roman Empire, the "economic backbone" of both societies. Yet he also states —which is the true picture—that ". . . the natives [of Hellenistic Egypt and Syria were] the economic backbone of the two countries"; that the "slaves were the backbone of the economic life of the [Roman] Empire. . . ."; that the "tenants and farmers formed its backbone"; and that the "peasants [of Roman Africa] . . . formed the vast majority of the popula-

tion and were the economic backbone of the country.". . .

. . . Rostovtzeff attributes the economic crisis in Italy in the first century A.D. to the emancipation of the provinces from dependence upon Italian products, which led to a decay of industry and commerce, the concentration of land in the hands of the imperial aristocracy and other Italian magnates, and the consequent ruin of "scientific agriculture." "In the crisis at the end of the first century the middle class was the first to suffer."

The steady concentration of land in fewer and fewer hands, with the gradual disappearance of small independent peasant landowners in the provinces as well as in Italy, is the leading economic development in the Roman Empire from the reign of Augustus on. "The tendency towards concentration of landed property in the hands of capitalists and city residents could not be stopped." From the very outset, and increasingly as time went on, the "urban bourgeoisie" attempted to solve the problem of the labor supply required to cultivate their landed estates by the institution of tenant small holders. In Rostovtzeff's view, the developing "scientific capitalistic agriculture" of the early Roman Empire was ruined by this practice. For the "urban bourgeoisie" withdrew their capital and management from their large-scale agricultural undertakings and became absentee landlords, living off income derived from less productive tenant farms. Since he holds the subjective view that an energetic and enterprising middle class developed a thriving "capitalism," that the primary source of the prosperity of his "urban bourgeoisie" of the early Roman Empire was commerce and industry, and that this class introduced the methods of "progressive and scientific farming" into agriculture as a supplementary field of investment, he is compelled to attribute the growth of absentee landownership (actually the dominant form of Roman economy) to a psychological transformation in the "urban bourgeoisie":

> This city-capitalism... gradually degenerated. The prevailing outlook of the municipal *bourgeoisie* was that of the *rentier:* the chief object of economic activity was to secure for the individual or for the family a placid and inactive life on a safe, if moderate, income.... The activity of the urban middle class degenerated into a systematic exploitation of the toiling lower classes. Its accumulated wealth was mostly invested in land. Commerce and industry became decentralized, and then they came to be pursued as a means of adding to an income derived mainly from agriculture.

The predominance of agriculture is thus for Rostovtzeff not the actual foundation of economic life, existing independently of the will, but a moral deviation of the ruling class, which, commencing with the end of the first century A.D., was affected by apathy, indolent contentment, and paralysis of energy. "Thus the impotence and idleness of the directing classes brought about a new social and economic crisis in the empire." "The result was the collapse of city-capitalism and the acute crisis of the third century, which brought about the rapid decline of business activity in general, the resuscitation of primitive forms of economy, and the growth of State-capitalism."

The "urban bourgeoisie," transformed by a changed attitude of mind from entrepreneurs into *rentiers*, became an exclusive minority:

> The existence of two castes, one ever more oppressed, the other ever more idle and indulging in the easy life of men of means, lay like an incubus on the Empire and arrested economic progress. All the efforts of the emperors to raise the lower classes to a working and active middle class were futile. The imperial power rested on the privileged classes, and the privileged classes were bound in a very short time to sink into sloth.

The stubborn opposition of the ruling class to the imperial policy of reviving a class of independent peasant smallholders resulted in a psychological change in the rural masses, whose century-old submissiveness flared up in the social revolution of the third century against the "urban bourgeoisie." "It was this [social] antagonism which was the ultimate cause of the crisis of the third century...."

Equally disastrous to sound (i.e., for Rostovtzeff, "capitalistic") economic development, and in part engendered by the selfish policy of the ruling class (for, as has been pointed out, he separates the state power from the ruling class), was the steadily mounting supremacy of the interests of the state over those of the entire population. The interference of the imperial government with "free enterprise," through progressively more burdensome taxation, through frequent requisitions, compulsory work and other forms of coercion, eventually even assaults on the "capital" of the "bourgeoisie," in order to solve economic problems and to meet the administrative and military requirements of the state, is at times regarded as the cause of the crisis of the third century A.D. and of the decay of the empire, affecting with apathy the ruling "bourgeoisie" as well as the masses.

It is to be noted that Rostovtzeff is cognizant of other fundamental factors, which, however, he regards as secondary:

that the "... weakest feature [of the Roman Empire] ... was the frailty of the foundations, especially the economic foundation, on which the whole fabric of the Empire rested"; that the economic system could support in comfort only a small minority, whose prosperity rested on intensive exploitation of the masses living on a bare subsistence level; that the wealth of the Empire was progressively drained by unproductive squandering of income and by exhausting military and administrative expenditures. But he insists on the psychological and social aspects as basic and primary: exclusiveness of the ruling "urban bourgeoisie" and consequent destructive hostility of the masses of peasants. The result of the overthrow of the "bourgeoisie" by civil war and direct assaults on their "capital" was a general social, economic, and intellectual levelling, the mutual ruin of both classes, universal impoverishment and decline of productivity, and the establishment of a bureaucratic state and an étatized economy. "This was the fatal blow to the aristocratic and urban civilization of the ancient world.". . .

Rostovtzeff's rejection of an economic interpretation as the basic explanation of the decline of ancient civilization is in keeping with his vigorously avowed, though inconsistently applied, pluralistic interpretation of history.

I cannot confidently speak of social and economic conditions as a *background* for the evolution of other manifestations of human life at any time or in any place. Social and economic conditions are as much aspects of human life as art, or any other field of human endeavor and human creative power. We may speak of inter-relations between these various manifestations, but not of dependence of one on the other. None of them may properly be spoken of as background for the others.

Rejecting a monistic interpretation of history, Rostovtzeff dismembers the development of society into the abstractions of independent historical factors. No one of the various spheres of historical phenomena—e.g., political, constitutional, artistic, social, economic, cultural, religious—is to be regarded as basic and decisive. All are equally important threads in the complex web of society, "indivisible from and closely correlated" with each other. Each branch of history, however, somehow retains its separate individuality, steering a relatively independent course, but developing along the same general lines as the others. Hence Rostovtzeff gives prominence now to one factor, now to another, with intuitive and deliberate arbitrariness and subjectivity, rarely attempting to examine the totality of all the opposing tendencies within a given historical phenomenon as a single, unified, mutually affecting process of evolution.

But it is only in part his pluralistic historical methodology which accounts for the glaring contradictions and inconsistencies in Rostovtzeff's judgments and conclusions. Equally responsible are his ambivalent petty-bourgeois ideological position, which beguiles him into viewing the same historical phenomenon from conflicting social aspects; an eclecticism that reflects the divergent and often irreconcilable evidence both in the primary sources and in the secondary works upon which he relies; and his subjective projection into antiquity of modern social and economic forms, which runs counter to the objective evidence well known to him.

Two of the historical "factors," the

economic and social, are conceived as forming a uniquely integrated group. And "... political and economic considerations are so closely connected that [it is] difficult to discriminate between them." And while he is especially careful to deny that the economic "factor" is the ultimate cause of historical phenomena, at times he treats it as primary and fundamental, determining the aspects of social and political life.

In general, however, social and economic conditions are separated in Rostovtzeff's method, and greater weight is assigned to the social "factor." This is seen even in his proposed order of treatment. The political aspect of any historical period is expounded first, then the social, and last the economic. This divorce of social forces from economic development and the deliberate treatment of social conditions before economic make it possible for Rostovtzeff, above all, to absolve the ruling classes of the Hellenistic world and the early Roman Empire, his idealized "bourgeoisie," of responsibility for economic crises and catastrophes. But it also explains his failure to achieve a consistent understanding of the dynamics of historical evolution, undistorted by subjective intrusions. "His society is thus, fundamentally, without direction, the product of contingency, and not a developing organism, for which 'social,' 'economic,' and 'political' are merely convenient categories to the historian who seeks to lay bare its processes of change."* His basic conclusion is the inevitable decay of society because of unchangeable traits of human nature.

* F. W. Walbank, *Classical Review*, 56 (1942), 84. Expanded note—Ed.

F. W. WALBANK (1909–), Rathbone Professor
of Ancient History and Classical Archaeology in
the University of Liverpool, published his *The Decline
of the Roman Empire in the West* at the end of
World War II. It reflects a justified detestation for
fascism and portrays the Empire as in the grip of a
tyrannical bureaucracy. There is an echo of
Rostovtzeff in Walbank's view that "the antagonism
of the classes" led to "the artificial creation of two
different kinds of human being" in the ruling minority
and the much larger numbers of the oppressed.*

F. W. Walbank

Shrinkage, Crisis, and
the Corporative State

To isolate the moment when a society
ceases to progress and begins to decay
is never easy. The factors involved are
so numerous, and concern phenomena
at such diverse stages of development,
that vigorous expansion in one sphere
may well coincide with already advanced
decay in another. But, if there is such
a moment in the history of the Roman
Empire, it falls in the year A.D. 117, when
Hadrian succeeded Trajan to the Principate.

Under Trajan the Empire achieved
its farthest territorial extension; now
Dacia beyond the Danube, Armenia and
Mesopotamia beyond the Euphrates,
were incorporated in the Empire. Trajan's primary objects were strategic; his

annexation of Dacia was the reply to
interference from its king, Decebalus,
who had forced Domitian to pay *dane-
geld*, while in his eastern policy he was
seeking a radical solution to the secular
conflict with Parthia. At the same time
this military policy coincided with the
general economic movement outwards.
For the classical area of trade was greater
than the Empire. The tendency towards
decentralisation had already resulted in
the splitting-up of a single oecumenical
trade system into a number of provincial
blocks, which were not, however, necessarily coterminous with the frontiers of
the Empire. Thus one block included
Greece, Macedonia, Thrace, Asia Minor
and Armenia, which were bound to-

---

* From F. W. Walbank, *The Decline of the Roman Empire in the West* (London, 1946),
38–57. Reprinted by permission of Lawrence & Wishart Ltd.

gether by ancient traditions and Hellenic culture; another embraced Syria, Babylon and Iran, an area half Roman and half Parthian in its political alignment. Sooner or later it was inevitable that the attempt should be made to unite blocks such as these within the political frontiers on the one side or the other; and it was this task which Trajan accomplished.

In doing so, however, he stretched the financial and military resources of the Empire to the breaking point; and Hadrian was quick to reverse this dangerous policy and, by relinquishing the territory beyond the Euphrates, to bring the Empire the relief which is reflected in the prosperity of the *pax Hadriani*. As a second Augustus, Hadrian toured the Empire, supervising its effective frontier dispositions and organising its provinces with wholly admirable solicitude. Yet by an ironical fate, the limit which he set to the expansion of the Empire proved in fact its death-warrant.

Its growth had been part of a process of political unification, corresponding to the economic unification of the ancient world; from that point of view Julius Caesar and Augustus were … the direct successors of Alexander the Great. It has been argued that, had he lived, Caesar meant to extend the frontiers yet further, and carry out Trajan's programme a century and a half before his time. Be that as it may, what is quite clear is that by the time of Trajan further expansion had become a task to which the resources of the Empire were no longer equal. In fact, Hadrian and his successors found themselves in a dilemma. The movement of economic decentralisation towards the periphery of the Empire furnished a constant incentive to extend the frontiers yet wider,

and to annex for Rome those areas which already enjoyed close commercial links with the Empire. In this way it might have been possible to open up yet further fields of foreign trade to compensate for that absence of a deep internal market which followed inevitably from the structure of ancient society. On the other hand, the disruptive influences which we have already examined above had, in the century and a half which divided Julius Caesar from Trajan, put any such development outside the range of practical politics.

Over the whole period from the first century to the time of Marcus Aurelius A.D. 161–180) there are clear indications of a fall in the population; a comparison of figures taken from Egypt and Palestine with the sums paid in connection with the manumission of slaves at Delphi during the same periods shows a general fall of prices alongside a rise in wages —phenomena which together confirm the general picture given in the literary sources of a universal decline in the population of the Empire. Moreover, as in Greece, during the crisis of the second century B.C., the bourgeoisie in particular were refusing to rear families. That this trend set in early is clear from the legislation which Augustus directed against it; and later emperors returned repeatedly to the problem. Equally, for reasons we must shortly consider, the bourgeoisie declined increasingly to accept their military responsibilities for the defense of the Empire; even the ordinary offices of administration which their ancestors had filled with pride now seemed a financial burden which they were loath to shoulder. In short, the resources and the manpower of the Empire were no longer adequate to the demands made upon them, still less to the pursuance of Trajan's policy of expansion, which was from many points of view the logical development of the Empire. The trends ... led in two opposite ways at once, posing the question of expansion, yet simultaneously reducing the capacity of society to carry it through. Such was Hadrian's dilemma; and though he and the Antonines after him responded to the challenge by retrenchment and consolidation, they could not in the long run save Roman society. . . .

For this monster* historians have had to find a name; and the names they have chosen are often revealing. Some have fallen back on the safe but colourless "étatisme"; others have called it "state-capitalism," a description at least partially correct; others again use the phrase "state-socialism," which is unsatisfactory because it ignores the social criterion in the modern theory of socialism—the happiness of the individual—a criterion which was completely absent from the Roman imperial system; and sometimes historians use both "state-socialism" and "state-capitalism" indiscriminately, a solution which indicates a confused conception of the economic and political institutions and theories of our times. Recently, however, the spread of fascism in Europe has rendered these artificial labels superfluous, by providing us with the true analogy of a bureaucratic police-state, based on oppression and the informer, and attempting the similar task of preserving an antiquated social system against the opposition of forces which have already rendered it virtually obsolete.

Perhaps, therefore, the most convenient title to use is that of the Corporative State, a term borrowed from Italian fascism, which has the merit of suggesting

* The state in the later Empire—Ed.

the special development which took place under the most forceful emperors of the period of chaos, Aurelian (A.D. 270–275), Diocletian (A.D. 284–305) and Constantine (A.D. 306–337). Their problem was to secure labour for the essential tasks of the Empire; and their answer was to develop as an instrument of state what had hitherto been a purely voluntary form of organisation.

Throughout the Hellenistic world, and especially in Ptolemaic Egypt, we find countless associations or guilds of people engaged in similar work; their functions were partly religious and partly those of the modern friendly society or burial club, and to some extent they protected the professional interests of their members, without ever approaching the status of the modern trade union. These *collegia,* as the Romans called them, had been frequently banned by the imperial government as potential sources of disorder; now it became evident that they could be incorporated in the official machinery. The change did not come all at once. After nationalising the corn supply of Rome, Augustus (27 B.C.–A.D. 14) had found it necessary to make special terms with the ship-masters (*navicularii*) and wholesale dealers (*negotiatores*) to ensure the regular arrival of the grain. The exchequer therefore offered special concessions to such individuals as would undertake to serve the government for six years. From the reign of Claudius (A.D. 41–54) onwards, the decline in the trade in goods for mass consumption became so considerable that men engaged in water transport usually had to combine this with some other occupation; accordingly, under Hadrian (A.D. 117–138) the State began to insist that a *navicularius* or *negotiator* should employ his full resources on state duties to secure the concessions offered.

As such arrangements assumed increasingly greater importance, the corporate bodies, or *collegia,* of the *navicularii* and *negotiatores* began to take the place of the individual traders in the contracts. Under Antoninus Pius (A.D. 138–161) the *navicularii* of Arles (who enjoyed special privileges, including a private office at Beyrout) were already functioning officially as a *collegium;* but it is not until the reign of Septimius Severus (A.D. 193–211) that a clear picture emerges of these specially privileged guilds —the smiths, the ship-owners and corn-traders, the oil merchants, the bakers and the pork-butchers—all operating at Rome, except for the *navicularii,* who formed a kind of Merchant Navy all over the Empire.

From now onwards the precedent of these privileged *collegia* governed official policy. Under Severus Alexander (A.D. 222–235) new guilds were established by direct state action; and Aurelian (A.D. 270–275) seems to have made guild-membership compulsory and hereditary for all trades at Rome. Gradually a system was growing up under which the State distributed basic rations of bread, wine, oil and pork either free or very cheaply, and in return exacted compulsory services from the guildsmen. By the fourth century A.D. the picture revealed by the legal codes is one of complete State control over the individual. Not only a few selected professions, but all trades and occupations are now organized in hereditary *collegia.* We hear, for example, of guilds of inn-keepers, fishmongers, potters and silversmiths; and there were similar organisations of public employees in the imperial post, the police, the grave-yards, the state textile-factories (of which there were seventeen producing fine materials in the west alone), and in the mints. Nor

did this apply merely to Rome; every town of any size had its own *collegia*— Aquileia, Lyons, Arles, Trier, Constantinople and Cyzicus, to mention but a few from which records have come down. Everywhere men were bound to their occupations. Those working in the mines and quarries and in the arms-factories were branded. By A.D. 403 bakers were forbidden to marry outside the families of their fellow-workers; and soon enrolment in the *collegia,* like enrolment in the *curiales,** appears as an official punishment for any criminal who has hitherto avoided "incorporation."

In this way the third century emperors carried out their task of preserving the Empire. Naturally they were resisted by the bourgeoisie, who, crushed between the upper and nether millstones of the State and an intractable proletariat, were being gradually squeezed out of existence. And this last struggle of the bourgeoisie "for what remained of political and spiritual freedom against the constraints of tyranny and dogma"[1] has aroused the sentimental sympathy of modern historians. This sympathy is very understandable. But we should not allow it to obscure our appreciation of what the Emperors achieved. Shrinking from no method, however oppressive, they succeeded by an almost superhuman effort in bringing the State through the crisis of the third century, and with it the heritage of Greece and Rome. Cribbed, cabined and confined, something of the classical world still lived on, to penetrate and modify every feature of the later western world that grew up on its ruins. Judged in the light of history, the later emperors performed an essential

* Local officials—Ed.

[1] Oertel in *Cambridge Ancient History,* Vol. XII, p. 268.

task and they performed it with great single-mindedness; in its accomplishment lay "the one last hope of all friends of civilisation."*

The characteristic constituent of the world they shaped was compulsion. It had to be a world in which every action of every individual was regulated. Monopolies made way for guilds: guilds hardened into castes. In A.D. 301 Diocletian attempted to fix prices and maximum wages throughout the Empire, with the death penalty for any breach of his edict. Everywhere men lived under military discipline, and did the tasks they were born to do. The world of free exchange and *laissez-faire* was utterly dead.

Besides regimenting and controlling, the Emperors also took more positive steps to supplement the failure and decay of private enterprise. Increasingly, the State itself began to enter into the industrial field; for by the beginning of the third century it was no longer possible to distinguish between the Emperor's economic activity as a private individual and direct participation by the State in commerce and industry. For some time the State (or Emperor) had been the largest landowner: now it became the largest owner of mines and quarries and the greatest industrialist. Originally it had entered industry to supply its own needs; mints, builders' yards, brick-kilns, textile-mills, iron-foundries and armourers' workshops had been established to meet the requirements of the court and, more especially, the army. But in the third and fourth centuries these enterprises were extended to meet the prevailing crisis, and were staffed by forced labour, recruited on a semi-military basis. The general pattern of this New Order

* F. M. Heichelheim, *Wirtschaftsgeschichte des Altertums*, vol. I (Leiden, 1938), p. 772. Expanded note—Ed.

was the ancient centralised monopoly State of Pharaonic or Ptolemaic Egypt; and even where the cottage system of industry still persisted, as in the case of certain weavers, the materials, obtained by a levy in kind, were doled out by the State in fixed amounts and the finished material duly collected according to a schedule.

This predominance of the State over the individual and his interests was in essence a reversion to oriental, Bronze Age methods of economic organisation. But—and this is important for an understanding of the issue—it was in no sense due to the application of a set of principles. The Emperors did not enter the economic field because they believed in State enterprise; their regulations were not the expression of an ideology favouring regimentation and state control. Hence it is misleading to see the issue as one of principle, as an ideological conflict between the State and the Individual. On the contrary, the later Caesars were the victims of circumstances, if ever men were. They found themselves faced with certain problems of finance and essential production, which could be solved in one way and one way only; and they went that way....

Such conditions as these only hastened and accentuated the flight to the countryside. We have already traced the growth of the large estates, each a nucleus around which craftsmen could assemble to form self-contained units, independent of the money economy now in disruption. As the demands of the central government upon the small craftsman or the independent peasant grew too severe, it was often with the large landowner that he could find his only refuge. For the landlords survived when the bourgeoisie perished. It is a mark of the primacy of land as the chief economic factor in the ancient world that the "racketeers" who naturally sprang up under the bureaucracy and in the chaos of the third century—men who flourished "not so much by virtue of their commercial ability and business energy, as the old bourgeoisie had done, but rather by unscrupulousness, extortion, bribery and the exploitation of the political constellation of the moment"[1]—put their wealth, not, like the Goerings and Cianos of our own times, into industry, but into land. Instead of industrial monopolists they became feudal barons.

The manor economy which thus grew up played an important cultural part in the history of the later Empire. The first impulse, which carried estate production even into the export market, proved a flash in the pan; but the manors continued to produce for the local market, thus fulfilling the function hitherto carried out by the towns. In this way the new, mediaeval orientation of the countryside towards the manor and its owner becomes more marked, and the relationship between the latter and the surrounding district intensified. Moreover, the manors were the chief remaining market for the international luxury trade, which continued to operate even after all primary needs were being satisfied locally. The rich landowners had the means to pay for spices from the east, elaborate woods and precious stones, which not being bulky still amply repaid the risks entailed in their shipment. Such manor houses, homes of luxury and culture even in the darkest hours of the Empire, stand out as the new guardians of the ancient tradition; and to some extent they bring culture to the countryside, with which they enjoy a more inti-

1 Oertel in *Cambridge Ancient History*, Vol. XII, p. 274.

mate relationship than was ever possible for the towns, whose place they have taken. A dissemination of culture at an infinitely lower level than had existed in the cities, but over a far wider area, was perhaps one of the more important positive achievements of this period.

Economically too the manorial household succeeded in bridging a gap which the classical economy had never managed to close—that between peasant proprietorship and the capitalistic plantation worked by slave labour. . . . [T]he general decline in the number of available slaves was accompanied by a depression in the status of the tenant-farmer, or *colonus*. Throughout the Empire, as agriculture fell back to subsistence levels, it became convenient to parcel out large estates among poor tenants or settlers, who paid the landlord with a fixed proportion of their yield and, in certain provinces (though not in Italy), with a stipulated amount of labour annually. This labour, reminiscent of the "socage" exacted from the mediaeval serf, was constantly being increased by the landlord (or, more often, by the rich tenant who came between the landlord and the *colonus*) with the connivance of the imperial officials; an African inscription of the second century A.D. has survived, in which certain tenants, "rustics of small means, winning a livelihood by the work of their hands," as they describe themselves, celebrate an unexpected legal victory in resisting just such a demand.

These small tenants were originally free men, bound only by their respective contracts. But from the time of Marcus Aurelius (A.D. 161–180) the Emperors began to replenish the depleted fields of the Empire with German settlers, often taken from among those defeated in war, and these *inquilini*, as they were termed, though for many purposes they ranked as free men, were legally tied to their plots of land. Not unnaturally the distinction between the free Roman *colonus* and the unfree Romanised *inquilinus* soon began to become blurred; and, as might be expected, it was the status of the *colonus* which deteriorated. Diocletian (A.D. 284–305) paved the way for the legal identification of the classes with a rescript which laid down the quantity of foodstuffs for the production of which each estate throughout the Empire was liable, based on the number of "heads of male labour" employed, no matter what their status. It now became a matter of imperial policy to grant the landowner the sanction to detain a tenant, for whose allotted quota of tax he was personally liable. Consequently on October 30th, A.D. 332, Constantine made the attachment of the tenant farmer to the manorial estate enforceable at law. Henceforth any *colonus* who fled was to be brought back in chains like a runaway slave.

Once established, the principle of compulsion grew rapidly. During the fourth century A.D. any peasants who still remained independent were also tied to their land and so reduced to effective serfdom. By A.D. 400 the legal codes speak of the peasants as virtually enslaved to the land on which they are born. More and more they are oppressed in the interests of their former landlords, now their masters; and a stream of legalisation defines ever more closely the terms of their subjection.

The Emperors viewed this growth in the power of the landlords with mixed feelings. It placed them in a dilemma. They might attempt to enrol the landlords in the service of the State by such regulations as that of Valens (A.D. 364–378), which made them responsible for the collection of all the taxes for which

their *coloni* were liable. At the same time it was recognised that the growth of the landlords was essentially a symptom of the breakdown of the State. Everywhere the colonate was constantly being recruited from the ranks of the independent peasants whom hard times drove to throw themselves on the mercy of the local landlord, surrendering their freedom in exchange for his patronage and protection. In A.D. 368 this practice was declared illegal by the same emperor Valens, who thus sought simultaneously to check and utilise an inevitable but ultimately disruptive institution. In fact the great landlords throve against the State and usurped its functions. Thus we find them along the northern frontiers, or in Africa, raising private armies of slaves—forerunners of the Mamelukes and Janissaries of the Ottoman Empire—to carry out frontier defence, and expelling the barbarian alone. But in the long run, by weakening the central authority, the manorial system weakened defence too, and so accelerated the disruption of the Empire. Meanwhile it helped in the general process by which the population of the Empire crystallised into the various social classes, each with its duties carefully defined in the new body of legislation which sprang up to give full sanction to the Corporative State.

These gradings, which form the essence of the later mediaeval world, begin to appear during the first three centuries A.D. and find their full legal authority in the fourth. The old categories of *cives Romani*, freedmen, slaves and the like, no longer exist. Instead, the whole population of the Empire is divided into *honestiores*,* who include the Emperors, the (Christian) priesthood and the new landed proprietors, together with officers,

* Men of high birth—Ed.

civil servants and the few big families of the towns, and *humiliores,* who include ultimately everyone else, whether serf or slave, craftsman or peasant. For these two grades there are separate functions, separate privileges and separate punishments; the antagonism of the classes has once more reached its logical end in the artificial creation of two different kinds of human being.

This structure, stable, simplified and primitive, was what came out of the Empire. Under this system the legacy of the ancient world was transmitted to later times. Meanwhile the real classical world had perished in the west. The barbarian invasions found little real resistance in a world already torn within, decentralised and irreparably weakened both socially and economically. The transfer of the capital to Byzantium in A.D. 330 meant the virtual division of the Empire. In A.D. 410 Alaric the Visigoth sacked Rome; and in A.D. 476 Odoacer liquidated a bankrupt concern by deposing Romulus Augustulus, the last western Emperor. In the east the Empire continued to exist as a bulwark of Christendom till A.D. 1453, though after the reign of Justinian (A.D. 527–565) it fell upon days almost as evil as those which had destroyed the west. "A so-called Imperial Government in Constantinople which had to look on helplessly while a Slav population supplanted a Latin and Greek population in the Balkan Peninsula, and an improvised system of army-corps districts replaced the Diocletianic provincial system in Anatolia, cannot be regarded as a real Government in any significant sense of the words."[1]

However, with the Eastern Empire we are not here concerned. Endowed with

an urban culture far more deeply rooted than that of the western provinces, and with a military reservoir of semi-civilised man-power in the hills of Asia Minor, it enjoyed sufficient advantages to enable it to weather the darkest days. Its achievements too were far from negligible; but they lay rather in the field of preservation and the maintenance of equilibrium, than in any new and vigorous undertaking. The question whether Byzantium should be treated as the true continuation of the Roman Empire, or regarded (as Toynbee regards it) as a "successor-state" similar to the Gothic kingdoms or Charlemagne's Empire in the west, is indeed ultimately one of terminology. There was continuity and there was also some degree of change. Justinian, the codifier of Roman Law, took an important step to further commerce when he introduced silk manufacture from the far east; and from the sixth to the eleventh century Byzantium remained the greatest trading power in Christendom. Yet throughout these centuries the legacy of the Roman Empire, as we have analysed it, was palpably clear. Byzantium remained a rigid caste-state, its rural districts largely desolate and its agriculture feeble, with neither the economic foundations nor the mental atmosphere to foster scientific thought and progress. It was a portent when in A.D. 1204 Constantinople fell to the marauders of the Fourth Crusade, who held it till A.D. 1265. In A.D. 1453, with the capture of the city by the Turks, the Eastern Empire at last came to an end. By this time its work of preservation was done. The very rise of its trade-rivals in the cities of Italy, which largely contributed to its decay and finally undermined its century-long resistance, . . . signified that the main stream of progress was once more advancing in the west.

[1] Arnold J. Toynbee, *A Study of History,* Vol. IV, Oxford, 1939, p. 328.

NORMAN H. BAYNES (1877–1961) was Bury's successor as the leading British historian of the Byzantine Empire, and, like Bury, he acted as an editor for the *Cambridge Ancient History*. In the lecture reprinted here he answers some modern theories on the fall of Rome (including those of Huntington and Tenney Frank) and proposes his own "humiliatingly simple" explanation. *

Norman H. Baynes

Some Modern Explanations[1]

It is the purpose of this paper to consider a few of the more outstanding contributions towards the solution of this familiar problem propounded since the publication in 1898 of Sir Samuel Dill's book on *Roman Society in the last century of the Western Empire* (2nd edn., 1899). It may well appear somewhat surprising that I should venture to speak on such a topic, since my own work, such as it is, has been concerned rather with the history of the Byzantine Empire. And yet for a student of Byzantine his-

tory the problem has a special interest: he is forced to consider that problem not merely as a West European issue, but rather to compare and contrast the historical development in the western and eastern provinces of the Empire. He is compelled to raise the question: why was it that the Roman Empire failed to survive in Western Europe while it endured for a further millennium in the East? The very fact that he is primarily interested in the history of the Byzantine Empire enables him to approach the Western problem from a different angle and to treat that problem in a wider setting and not in isolation. That is my apologia for what might

[1] Read at the Joint Meeting of the Hellenic and Roman Societies on Friday, 4th September, 1942. This paper originally formed part of the Sir Samuel Dill Memorial Lecture delivered in Belfast on 27th January, 1933.

* From "The Decline of the Roman Power in Western Europe. Some Modern Explanations," *Journal of Roman Studies*, 33 (1943), 29–35. Reprinted by permission of the Society for the Promotion of Roman Studies, copyright reserved.

otherwise appear to be an inexcusable impertinence. In a word I desire to ask what general considerations can be adduced to explain the fact that in Western Europe there is a cultural break—a caesura—while in the East Roman world the cultural development is continuous, the Hellenistic and Roman traditions being gradually fused to form the civilisation of the Byzantine Empire.

Of the recent explanations of the decline of the Roman power in Western Europe we may first take that of Vladimir G. Simkhovitch who in the *Political Science Quarterly* for 1916 published an article under the title "Rome's Fall Reconsidered"[2] in which he attributed the collapse of the Roman power to the exhaustion of the soil of Italy and of the provinces. That article has been reprinted — somewhat incongruously — in the author's book *Towards the Understanding of Jesus*.[3] The evil began under the Republic: in Cato's time agriculture had already declined in the greater part of Italy. When asked what is the most profitable thing in the management of one's estate he replied "Good pasturage." What is the next best? "Fairly good pasturage." What is the third best? "Bad pasturage." And the fourth best? "Arare" —agriculture. Simkhovitch admits that the Romans possessed great agricultural knowledge. "All that is implied by the agricultural revolution," he writes, "the seeding of grasses and legumes, the rotation of crops, yes even green manuring, all that was perfectly known to the Romans. Why was it not practised for two thousand years or more? I do not know." Columella was already drawing upon a

2 *Political Science Quarterly* xxxi (1916), 201–243.

3 *Towards the Understanding of Jesus* (New York: The Macmillan Company, 1937), pp. 84–139.

literary tradition in his counsel to farmers: his mistakes prove that he had never witnessed the operations which he describes. To seed alfalfa one cyathus for 50 square feet, which amounts to several bushels per acre, is an impossible proposition. Province after province was turned by Rome into a desert: draining was neglected, and deserted fields became mosquito- and malaria-infested swamps. The "inner decay" of the Roman Empire in all its manifold manifestations was in the last analysis entirely based upon the endless stretches of barren, sterile, and abandoned fields in Italy and the provinces. The evidence adduced by Simkhovitch is drawn for the most part from writers of the Republic or of the period of the early Principate, but from the Christian Empire he quotes Constantine's legislation in favour of the children of the poor who have not the means to provide for their offspring, and also the constitution of Valentinian, Arcadius and Theodosius giving permission to the squatter to cultivate deserted fields. Against those who would maintain that the flight from the land was caused by oppressive taxation he contends that it was precisely the exhaustion of the soil which rendered the burden of taxation oppressive: it was because so much land was uncultivated that taxation pressed so heavily upon those who still continued the farming of their fields. The limits which confine the productivity of man's labour become for society physical conditions of existence from which it cannot escape. It was these limits set by the exhaustion of the soil which rendered the doom of Rome inevitable.

There is no doubt truth in this picture of the decline of agriculture: for the later Empire it may well be an accurate description of some parts of Italy: in A.D. 395 the abandoned fields of Campania alone amounted to something over 528,-000 *jugera*;* but in itself it is inadequate as an explanation of the fall of Rome. For in one country at least—Egypt—there can be no question of soil-exhaustion, and it is precisely from Egypt that we have our earliest reports of the flight from the land, of the disappearance of villages through depopulation. Modern studies of economic conditions in Egypt have demonstrated the fatal effects of the methods of administrative exploitation employed by the Roman government in that province. The burden of taxation here certainly came first, and the decay of agriculture was its result and not its cause. Further, the sweeping generalisations of Simkhovitch's paper cannot be sustained: even in the fifth century of our era where a resident proprietor supervised the cultivation of his own estate there can be no question of soil-exhaustion. Read again Ausonius' poem of his expedition in the valley of the Moselle, read the letters of Sidonius Apollinaris: still in the Gaul of the fifth century it is clear that there were smiling fields and well-cultivated farms. The real danger of the *latifundia* lay, I am convinced, in the fact that they were for the most part managed by bailiffs for owners who were absentee landlords, men who drew money from their estates in order to spend it in Rome, Ravenna, or some provincial capital. The primary cause of the agricultural decline is to be found in the abuses of the fiscal system, in the scourge of corporate responsibility for the collection of the taxes which ruined the municipal aristocracy of the city *curiae*, and perhaps above all in the absence of the personal supervision of the proprietor and the unprincipled use of authority by irresponsible bailiffs, controlling the cultivation of the large estates which now absorbed so great a part of the land of the empire. Soil-exhaustion is, in fact, an inadequate explanation of the collapse of the Roman power.

Another theory has been proposed by Professor Ellsworth Huntington—that of climatic change.† The great sequoias of California—the big trees of a familiar advertisement—have been growing for some three or even four thousand years. Each year in the trunk of the tree there is clearly marked the circle of the year's growth: when the tree is felled these rings can be traced and according to their width a chronological chart of climatic variation can be established: the years of considerable width of ring recording the effect of favourable climatic conditions, the narrower rings marking the result of less favourable climate. In this way for the area of the sequoias the variations in climate can be traced for at least 3,000 years. On this basis Ellsworth Huntington constructed his theory. In an article published in 1917 in the *Quarterly Journal of Economics* on "Climatic Change and Agricultural Exhaustion as Elements in the Fall of Rome"[4] he suggested that the climate

* One *jugerum* is rather more than half an acre—Ed.

† See above, pp. 55–61.

[4] On climatic change and the evidence of tree-growth, *cf.* Ellsworth Huntington, "The Secret of the Big Trees," *Harper's Monthly Magazine* cxxv (American Edition), lxiv (European Edition), 292–302 (July, 1912); *id.*, "Climatic Change and Agricultural Exhaustion as Elements in the Fall of Rome," *Quarterly Journal of Economics* (Harvard University Press) xxxi (February, 1917), 173–208; Carnegie Institute of Washington, *Publication No.* 192 (1914, pp. vi, 341); Ellsworth Huntington, with contributions by Charles Schuchert, Andrew E. Douglass, and Charles J. Kullmer, "The Climatic Factor as illustrated in

of the Mediterranean world and that of California have always undergone similar modifications: that from the chronological chart of Californian climate one is accordingly entitled to reconstruct the changes in the climate of the Mediterranean area during the course of the history of Rome, and from the record of such changes we may conclude that the fall of Rome was due to a decline in the rainfall from which the Mediterranean world suffered during the fourth, fifth, and sixth centuries of our era. It is easy to object that on Professor Huntington's own showing the latter part of the second century and the first half of the third century marked a climatic improvement: it might be hard to trace any corresponding increase in prosperity in the history of the Empire during this period. But a more serious objection would point to the hazardous character of the fundamental assumption. Records of rainfall in the neighbourhood of the great trees have only been kept for about half a century; Professor Huntington prints a table of four year-groups in order to establish the climatic parallelism between California and the Mediterranean area (*Quarterly Journal of Economics* xxxi, 1916–17, 193):

I.   Seven years of heaviest rainfall in California.

II. Eighteen years with heavy rainfall in California.

III. Seventeen years with light rainfall in California.

arid America"; *Publication No.* 289 in three volumes: A. E. Douglas, "Climatic Cycles and Tree Growth. A Study of the Annual Rings of Trees in relation to Climate and Solar Activity" (vol. i, 1919, pp. 127, Bibliography 124–7; vol. ii, 1928, pp. vii, 166, Bibliography 159–166); "Climatic Cycles and Tree Growth" (vol. iii, 1936, pp. vii, 171, Bibliography 166–171); *Publication No.* 352 (1925) on "Quaternary Climates," Ernest Antevs, "The Big Tree as a Climatic Measure" 115–153, Bibliography 150–3.

IV. Thirteen years with least rainfall in California.

The table presents the following figures:

	San Francisco	Rome	Naples
I.	8.3 in.	10.7 in.	11.5 in.
II.	4.5 in.	10.6 in.	11.0 in.
III.	3.4 in.	9.8 in.	9.2 in.
IV.	1.9 in.	9.6 in.	8.6 in.

"The columns vary," writes Professor Huntington, "in harmony with the California rainfall." That is true, but the disparity in the amount of the decline in rainfall between California and Rome —in California a fall from 8.3 in. to 1.9 in., in Rome a fall only from 10.7 in. to 9.6 in.—is very striking, and it is not easy to see what conclusions can justifiably be drawn from such figures.

But that is not all: the matter does not remain as it stood in 1917. In 1925 the Carnegie Institute of Washington published further discussion of the Big Tree as a climatic measure, and it now appears uncertain what part is played respectively by temperature and what by rainfall in the yearly growth. Thus a further element of ambiguity is introduced into the problem. Before this Ossa of doubt piled upon a Pelion of uncertainty the confidence of a mere student of history may well quail, and for the present I should hesitate to call in aid Nature's yardstick as a solution of our historical perplexities. The great trees still keep their climatic secret.

From Nature we may turn to the human factor in our search for the causes of the collapse of the Roman power. Otto Seeck has, I think, found no followers in his attempt to charge the third-century Roman emperors with the responsibility for that collapse. Through their continued *Ausrottung der*

Besten—the persistent extermination of capacity and individual merit—the Caesars bred a terror of distinction and encouraged the spread of that slave mentality which issued logically and naturally in the triumph of Christianity —the Beggars' Religion—*die Religion des Betteltums*. An inverted Darwinism stamped out originality from the Empire: no man remained with the courage to be the master of his fate—the captain of his own soul. The way was open for "Byzantinismus," for crawling servility and fawning adulation of authority. Here the prejudice of one who was inspired by a passionate and life-long hatred of the Christian faith has, I cannot but feel, attempted to wrest history to its own purpose. Is there indeed any single century in the annals of the Empire which can show so many men of outstanding personality as can the fourth century of our era? Surely Professor Lot is not far from the truth when he exclaims: "If ever there were supermen in human history they are to be found in the Roman emperors of the third and fourth centuries"—men who shouldered the burden of a tottering world and resolutely refused to despair of the Republic. And beside the Roman emperors stand in the Christian camp such figures as Athanasius and S. Basil in the East, as Ambrose and Augustine in the West. There is little of crawling servility in such men as these. The wonder of the fourth century to my mind is rather the heroic courage and the desperate resolution with which men strove to preserve that imperial organisation which alone safeguarded the legacy of the ancient world. Further, you will not have failed to notice with what rigour Seeck presses the theory of the hereditary transmissibility of ἀρετή.*

* "excellence"—Ed.

So thorough-going a conviction might well rejoice the heart of a champion of an unreformed House of Lords. No, *Die Ausrottung der Besten* will not suffice to explain the decline of the Roman power.

Professor Tenney Frank, of the Johns Hopkins University, Baltimore, has approached the problem from another angle.† From an elaborate statistical study of the Corpus of Latin inscriptions[5] he concludes that Rome and the Latin West were flooded by an invasion of Greek and Oriental slaves: as these were emancipated and thus secured Roman citizenship the whole character of the citizen body was changed: on the basis of a consideration of some 13,900 sepulchral inscriptions he argues that nearly 90 per cent of the Roman-born inhabitants of the Western capital were of foreign extraction. What lay behind and constantly reacted on those economic factors which have generally been adduced to explain the decline of the Roman power was the fact that those who had built Rome had given way to a different race. "The whole of Italy as well as the Romanized portions of Gaul and Spain were during the Empire dominated in blood by the East." In this fact Tenney Frank would find an explanation of the development from the Principate to the Dominate—the triumph of absolutism, of the spread of Oriental religions, the decline in Latin literature and the growing failure in that gift for the government of men which had built up the Empire.

But the foundations on which this far-reaching theory rests are not above suspicion. The nationality of Roman slaves

† See above, pp. 47–54—Ed.
[5] "Race Mixture in the Roman Empire," *American Historical Review* xxi, 1916, 689 ff.; see also by him *An Economic History of Rome* 1927, 207 ff., 211 ff.

is but rarely expressly stated in the sepulchral inscriptions, and thus it is upon the appearance of a Greek name for slave or freedman that Tenney Frank has inferred an Oriental origin. The legitimacy of this inference has been questioned by Miss Mary Gordon in her able study of the "Nationality of Slaves under the early Roman Empire," JRS* xiv, 1924. A slave was a personal chattel, and slave-dealer or slave-owner could give to the slave any name which in his unfettered choice he might select: the slave dealers with whom Romans first came in contact were Greeks and thus, as Miss Gordon says, "Greek was the original language of the slave trade and this is reflected in servile nomenclature much as the use of French on modern menus and in the names affected by dressmakers suggests the history and associations of particular trades." In fact, the nomenclature of the slave in the ancient world was scarcely less arbitrary than are the modern names given to our houses, our puddings, our horses or our dogs. An attempt to determine the domicile of origin of our cats or dogs solely by the names which their owners have given them would hardly be likely to produce results of high scientific value. The outlandish names of barbarian captives reduced to slavery would naturally be changed to more familiar forms, and Latin nomenclature was singularly poor and unimaginative: the Greek names were well-known and resort to these was easy. It may be said that this reasoning is largely a priori and of little cogency. But Ettore Cicotti in a recent paper on "Motivi demografici e biologici nella rovina della civiltà antica" in Nuova Rivista storica, Anno xiv, fasc. i–ii, has adduced an interesting historical

* Journal of Roman Studies—Ed.

parallel. L. Livi (La schiavitù domestica nei tempi di mezzo e nei moderni, Ricerche storiche di un antropologo, Roma, 1928) in 1928 published documents which his father copied from the State Archives of Florence. These documents record 357 sales of slaves: the transactions date from the years 1366 to 1390—for the most part from the years 1366 to 1370. The majority of the slaves were of Tartar origin, though some were Greeks, Roumanians, etc. In these records the slave's original name is generally given and then follows the Italian name by which the slave is known. Thus the name of Lucia occurs forty-two times and represents such original names as Marchecta, Gingona, Erina, Minglacha, Saragosa, Casabai, Alterona and many others. Similarly the name of Caterina is given to slaves of Greek, Tartar, Turkish, Circassian, and Russian origin and has taken the place of such barbarous names as Coraghessan, Chrittias, Colcatalo, Tagaton, and Melich. The parallel is very instructive.

But this is not all: the sepulchral inscriptions studied by Tenney Frank extend over a period of three centuries: suppose that Rome had during the early Empire a population of some 800,000 with an annual mortality of 20 per cent: in those three centuries the deaths would number 4,800,000. Tenney Frank has examined 13,900 inscriptions and those are derived from imperial and aristocratic columbaria: here the slaves would be better off and the percentage of accomplished foreign slaves would be higher: what of the nameless dead whom no record preserved, whose bodies lay in the vast common burial pits of the slave proletariat? These 13,900 dead who left permanent memorials behind them cannot be regarded as really representative of the general servile population of the city: we are not justified in using the percentage obtained from these records and applying it as though it were applicable to the whole class of slaves and of freedmen.

In the light of this criticism Tenney Frank's statistics are vitiated, and it must be admitted that the nationality of the slaves of Rome under the early Empire remains a matter of conjecture. There must have been a far greater number derived from Western Europe than are allowed for on Tenney Frank's calculations.

A somewhat different form of biological explanation is given by Professor Nilsson in his well known book *Imperial Rome*. The most important problem for the Empire was that of race: that was decisive, for upon it depended the quality of Roman civilisation. Culture rests on racial character. If the alien races and barbarian peoples were to be assimilated, they must be interpenetrated by their conquerors. Since the Roman world was of vast extent and those of alien race were very numerous, an increase in the birth-rate of the Romans was required: instead of this the Roman birth-rate declined: the blood of the Romans became more and more diluted, and in place of the Romanisation of the Empire a civilisation of intercommunication and intercourse resulted in a mingling of races—an unchecked "mongrelisation." Under the Empire cross-breeding, hybridisation, spread throughout the provinces and in this widespread realm of mongrels all stable spiritual and moral standards were lost.

I confess that as soon as the word "race" is introduced into any discussion I realise that my only safe course lies in a resolute silence, for I. have never been able to understand the precise significance of that ambiguous term. But when folk begin to ascribe all kinds of moral and spiritual failings to race-mixture it will hardly be expected that an Englishman will accept the insinuation without a protest. It is beyond calculation to estimate how many races and peoples have gone to his ethnological make-up, and he will not readily admit that the results of "mongrelisation" have in his case been wholly deplorable. As an Englishman I am unlikely to discuss dispassionately the theory of Professor Nilsson. And unfortunately I am also a student of Byzantine history and as such I am convinced that the essential condition of the prosperity of the later Roman Empire was its possession of Asia Minor —that reservoir alike of money and of men. And Asia Minor of the Byzantines was surely man's most stupendous effort in race-mixture to which history can point: it was an ethnological museum. Professor Nilsson, to be quite frank, will have his work cut out to persuade an English Byzantinist that race-mixture is of necessity so poisonous and deadly a process. I had better leave it at that: you had best form your own judgment on the theory without further comment from me.

There still remains, however, the explanation of Professor Rostovtzeff as set forth in his *Social and Economic History of the Roman Empire,* a masterpiece for which any student of imperial Rome must have a sincere admiration. Professor Rostovtzeff's explanation of the collapse of the Roman power can be briefly summarized.* It was through the medium of the *municipia*—of the towns—that Rome had unified Italy, and when she extended her conquests into the West

* See above, pp. 69–75—Ed.

of Europe she naturally favoured the growths of towns as centres of Romanisation. But the towns drew their wealth from the countryside, and the peasants bitterly resented this exploitation of their own class by the *bourgeoisie*. Under the peace of the Empire the civilian population became unfitted for the life of the military camps, and it was from the rude vigour of the peasantry that in the crisis of the third century the Roman armies were recruited. The peasant of the army made common cause with the peasant of the countryside and both waged a war of extermination against their oppressors of the city. The explanation of the downfall of the aristocracy and with them of the ancient civilisation is thus to be found in a class-conscious alliance between the soldier and the worker on the land. Professor Rostovtzeff, it must be remembered, has seen in his native country an aristocratic régime overthrown by a similar alliance. And the only answer to this theory that I can give is quite simply that I can find no support for it in our extant sources. I have consulted every reference to the authorities cited by Professor Rostovtzeff and in my judgment none of them supports his reading of the facts. So far as I can see the constant terror of the peasants is the soldier: the last menace to a defaulting debtor is (according to the papyri) the creditor's threat: "I will send a soldier after you." The soldier is to the peasant what Napoleon or the policeman has been to successive generations of children in English nurseries. To the Roman peasant and soldier of the third century of our era there had not been granted a revelation of the gospel according to Karl Marx.

And thus I come back as a student of Byzantine history to the difficulty to which I referred at the beginning of this lecture. I believe that there was in Western Europe a break in the cultural development and that there was no corresponding break in the development of civilisation in the eastern provinces of the Roman Empire. To a Byzantinist, therefore, the problem which we are considering necessarily assumes a dual aspect: what he must discover, if he is to gain any intellectual satisfaction from the inquiry, is precisely the *differentia* which distinguishes the history of the Western provinces from that of the *partes orientales*. And so many of the modern explanations do not provide him with any such *differentia*. "Die Ausrottung der Besten," civil wars, and imperial jealousy of outstanding merit did not affect the West alone: the whole Roman world suffered from these scourges: the brutality of an undisciplined soldiery was likewise an evil common to both halves of the Empire. Soil-exhaustion, climatic change, these must have affected the entire Mediterranean area. The oppression of civil servants, the decay of the municipal senates, the flight from the land—all these ills the Eastern provinces were not spared. Greeks and Orientals invaded the West and we are told caused the collapse of the Roman power there; but in the East these same Greeks and Orientals sustained the Empire against unceasing assaults for another millennium: it seems mysterious. And therefore in closing it only remains for me to state the *differentia* as I see it and to suggest an explanation of this diversity in the history of East and West—an explanation which is so humiliatingly simple that I am constrained to believe that it must be right.

You realise then that I speak as a student of Byzantine history: a Byzantinist looks at the world of Western Europe. As I conceive of it, culture is essentially a social thing: it is born of intercourse and it needs a conscious solidarity of interest in order to sustain it. Roman civilisation depended upon intercommunication, upon the influences radiating from the capital and returning to the capital for reinforcement. Such free communication, however, can be preserved only within an area which is safeguarded from violence: the Roman Empire was such an area safeguarded by the civil administration and by the frontier screen of the military forces. The civil service and the army together formed the steel framework which maintained the entire structure of civilisation. It is perhaps with the Emperor Hadrian that one first observes a conscious realisation of this function of the Roman power. The area of civilisation is delimited on permanent lines: not expansion of territory but concentration of resources in order to protect the solidarity of culture—that is the emperor's task. The barbarian invasions broke into this area of intercourse, and the establishment of barbarian kingdoms on Roman soil destroyed the single administration which was its counterpart. And the fatal significance of the establishment of these barbarian kingdoms lay in the fact that they withdrew from the Empire not only Roman soil, but also the revenues derived therefrom. Africa lost to the Vandals, Spain occupied by Sueve and Alan and Visigoth: Southern France a Visigothic kingdom and the rest of Gaul a battleground on which Aëtius fought and fought again: Italy alone remained as a source of revenue, and Italy was an impoverished land. The Western state was bankrupt. And the defence of the Empire demanded money, for Rome had so effectually provided the area of peaceful intercourse in Western Europe that her subjects were no longer soldiers: if battles were to be won they must be fought by barbarian mercenaries and for mercenaries to fight they must be paid. Further, Rome's effort in the West was a struggle with a double front: against the barbarian on land and against the Vandal fleet upon the sea. Rome possessed no technical superiority such as the invention of gunpowder might have given her, such as later the secret for the composition of the "Greek fire" gave to the Byzantine navy. Thus the tragedy of the Empire in the West lay precisely in the fact that she had not the wherewithal to keep at one and at the same time a mercenary army in the field and a fleet in commission. And the *differentia* which distinguishes the situation in the East of the Empire is in my judgment that, while the Danubian provinces were continuously ravaged, Asia Minor was for the most part untroubled by invasions: Asia Minor remained as I have said a reservoir alike of men and money. It was this reservoir which the West lacked. The West could throw no counterpoise into the scale against the supremacy of the barbarian; but the East amongst its own subjects numbered the hardy mountaineers—the Isaurians—and the fellow-countrymen of the Isaurian Tarasicodissa, whom history knows as the Emperor Zeno, could meet the menace of the barbarian mercenary and when the supremacy of the Alan Aspar had been broken, the Empire could send the Isaurian back to his mountains and Anastasius, an aged civilian who had only just escaped consecration as a bishop, could rule unchallenged. And as a consequence of the triumph of the civil power, the civil administration—the steel frame-work which maintained Byzantine civili-sation—was likewise preserved, and from the city of Constantine culture radiated and through intercourse with the capital was again reinforced. Here is preserved that conscious solidarity in the mainte-nance of civilisation which guaranteed a real continuity. In the West there are survivals from the ancient world—true—a branch lopped from a tree may still produce shoots; but for all that the con-tinuity of life is broken: the doom of decay is sure. Gregory of Tours is a remarkable man, but he is a lonely figure and he feels himself isolated. And against that figure I would set a scene at a Byzantine court—when the Emperor's barbarian mistress appeared in her radi-ant beauty at a reception, one courtier uttered the words οὐ νέμεσις:* the bar-barian queen did not understand the allusion, but for Byzantines the two words were enough to summon up the picture of Helen as she stood before the greybeards on the walls of Troy. So well did the aristocracy of East Rome know their Homer: such is the solidarity of Byzantine culture. In a word it was the pitiful poverty of Western Rome which crippled her in her effort to main-tain that civil and military system which was the presupposition for the continued life of the ancient civilisation.

* "There can be no blame": a reference to Homer, *Iliad* 3.156, where some Trojan elders see Helen and remark that no one could blame the Trojans and Greeks for fighting over such a woman. The anecdote is told by Michael Psellos, *Chronographie* (ed. Renauld), vol. I, p. 146—Ed.

A. H. M. JONES (1904–1970), the Professor of
Ancient History in the University of Cambridge, was a
scholar of prodigious scope. His *The Later Roman
Empire* is the most ambitious history of this period in
English since the books of J. B. Bury. In the excerpt
printed here (from a shortened version of this work),
Jones draws our attention back to the political and
military reasons for the fall of the Empire. His thesis
agrees at several points with that of Baynes (see
previous essay).*

A. H. M. Jones

Why Did the Western Empire Fall?

The causes of the fall of the western empire in the fifth century have been endlessly debated since Augustine's day, but those who have debated the question have all been westerners, and have tended to forget that the eastern empire did not fall till many centuries later. Many of the causes alleged for the fall of the west were common to the east, and therefore cannot be complete and self-sufficient causes. If, as the pagans said in 410, it was the gods, incensed by the apostasy of the empire, who struck it down, why did they not strike down the equally Christian eastern parts? If, as Salvian argues, it was God who sent the barbarians to chastize the sinful Romans,

why did He not send barbarians to chastize the equally sinful Constantinopolitans? If Christianity, as Gibbon thought, sapped the empire's morale and weakened it by internal schisms, why did not the more Christian east, with its much more virulent theological disputes, fall first?

We must look then for points in which the two halves of the empire differed. In the first place the western provinces were much more exposed to barbarian attack. The western emperor had to guard the long fronts of the Rhine and the upper Danube, the eastern emperor only the lower Danube. For on the eastern front his neighbour was the Persian empire, a

* From A. H. M. Jones, *The Decline of the Ancient World* (New York, 1966), 362–370. Reprinted by permission of Longmans, Green & Co. Ltd. and Holt, Rinehart and Winston, Inc.

101

civilized power which was not on the whole aggressive and kept its treaties. If a Persian war broke out, it was a more serious affair than a barbarian invasion, but wars were rare until the sixth century, and they then tested the Roman empire very severely. Moreover, if the western emperor failed to hold any part of the Rhine and Danube fronts, he had no second line of defence; the invaders could penetrate straight into Italy and Gaul, and even into Spain. The eastern emperor, if he failed, as he often did, to hold the lower Danube, only lost control temporarily of the European dioceses; for no enemy could force the Bosphorus and the Hellespont, guarded by Constantinople itself. Asia Minor, Syria and Egypt thus remained sealed off from invasion.

The barbarian invaders soon grasped the strategical position and, even if they first crossed the lower Danube and ravaged Thrace and Illyricum, soon tired of these exhausted lands and, unable to penetrate into the rich lands of Asia Minor, trekked westwards to Italy. This path was successively followed by the Visigoths under Alaric and the Ostrogoths under Theoderic.

In the second place the eastern parts were probably more populous, more intensively cultivated and richer than the western. This is hard to prove and difficult to believe nowadays, when the Balkans, Asia Minor and Syria are poor and thinly peopled, and only Egypt is rich and populous, whereas in the west Italy, France, Britain and the Low Countries are wealthy and densely populated, and only north Africa is poor. But many lines of argument suggest that the reverse was true in Roman times. The population of Egypt was about 8 million, that of Gaul (which included besides modern France the Low Countries and Germany west of

the Rhine) can be estimated at about 2½ million. The diocese of Egypt yielded perhaps three times as much revenue as that of Africa. Archaeological evidence proves that many areas now desert or waste in Syria and Asia Minor were inhabited and cultivated in late Roman times, and suggest that much of the most fertile soil in northern Gaul and Britain was still uncleared forest. It is moreover possible to estimate the wealth of different areas in the Roman empire from the number and scale of the public buildings of the cities, since the rich put much of their surplus wealth into such buildings. On this test the Mediterranean lands, eastern and southern Spain, southern Gaul, Italy, Africa, the southern Balkans, Asia Minor, Syria and Egypt were all wealthy, and Asia Minor and Syria the wealthiest of all, whereas Britain, northern Gaul and the Danubian lands were miserably poor, This analysis is borne out by literary testimonies. In the west Sardinia, Sicily and above all Africa, were regarded as the richest provinces, the granaries of the empire, and Aquitania as more fertile than northern Gaul. This implies that the potential fertility of the northern plains had not yet been exploited to the full.

In some other ways the east was superior to the west. It enjoyed much greater political stability and less of its resources were wasted in civil wars. From the accession of Diocletian in 284 to the death of Maurice in 602 there were only five attempted usurpations, those of Domitius Domitianus under Diocletian, of Procopius under Valens, of Basiliscus, Marcian and Leontius under Zeno, and all were quickly subdued without many casualties. In the west there were rebellions or usurpations by Carausius, Maxentius, Alexander, Magnentius, Firmus, Magnus Maximus, Gildo, Constantine,

Jovinus and John, most of which involved heavy fighting, and after the death of Valentinian III a succession of ephemeral emperors.

The social and economic structure of the east was healthier than that of the west. In the east more of the land was owned by peasant proprietors, who paid taxes only, and thus a larger proportion of the total yield of agriculture went to the peasantry. In the west a much higher proportion of the land was owned by great landlords, whose tenants had to pay rents in excess of their taxes, and the general condition of the peasantry was therefore poorer. This is reflected in the recurrent revolts of the Bacaudae in Gaul and Spain, which at times contained troops urgently needed elsewhere.

Another result of this difference in social structure was that the landed aristocracy in the west obtained a stranglehold on the administration, with two deleterious results. They were inefficient administrators, and allowed the bureaucracy to add a very appreciable sum to the burden of taxation by their exorbitant fees. They were over-indulgent to their own class, and slack in curbing grants of immunity and reductions and remissions of taxes. In the east the administrative machine remained in the hands of men of middle-class origin, who owed their advancement to the imperial government; they kept the expenses of tax collection down to a very reasonable figure, and periodically cancelled reductions of tax granted to landowners. A higher proportion of the total yield of agriculture thus reached the imperial treasury, and less was absorbed by the bureaucracy and by landlords.

Another question may be asked. When the western empire had stood firm for two-and-a-half centuries from the reign of Augustus, and had surmounted the crisis of the mid-third century, and, reorganized by Diocletian, had maintained itself intact for another three generations, why did it so rapidly collapse in the fifth century? Was the collapse primarily due to increased outside pressure or to internal decay or to a mixture of both?

One can only approximately gauge the external pressure on the empire. If one compares two historians who wrote on a similar scale of the first and of the fourth centuries A.D., Tacitus and Ammianus, one gains the impression that in the former period there was no heavy pressure on the frontiers, but in general peace, with only occasional border wars, whereas in the latter the emperors were constantly engaged in checking a breakthrough here and another breakthrough there. The first serious attack on the Roman frontier was under Marcus Aurelius, and in the mid-third century the migrations of the Goths and other east German tribes set up a general movement along the Danube, while the west German tribes grouped in the Frankish and Alamannic federation became more aggressive. The emperors of the late third century managed to restore the line, but it was henceforth held with far more effort than before. In the third quarter of the fourth century the westward movement of the Huns set all the German tribes in motion, and their pressure on the empire was redoubled. The tremendous losses incurred by the western Roman army during this period, amounting it would seem to two-thirds of its effectives, are striking evidence of the severity of the barbarian attacks.

One cause of weakness to the western parts was their administrative separation from the east. Formerly the emperors had been able to draw freely on the wealth of the east to finance the defence of the west. From the time of Diocletian the relatively poor western parts had to make do on their own resources with only occasional aid from the east.

To meet the increased barbarian pressure both halves of the empire enormously increased their armed forces, probably doubling their numbers. How far the high standard of military efficiency established in the principate was kept up, it is difficult to say, but it is unlikely that there was any significant decline. As any reader of Tacitus knows, the army of the early principate was not perfect. In peaceful times discipline became very slack, and the men spent their days on their private avocations and rarely attended a parade. Troops could get out of hand and plunder the provinces they were supposed to protect, and could panic in the face of the enemy. The officers were not professional soldiers and were often incompetent. These and other weaknesses appear in the later Roman empire, but the officers were on the whole of better quality, being experienced professionals. Small bodies of Roman troops still could and did defeat very much larger barbarian hordes in the fourth, fifth and sixth centuries.

The heavy economic burden imposed by the increased size of the army overstrained the resources of the empire and produced a number of weaknesses. It may seem an exaggeration to say that the resources of so large an area as the Roman empire could be overstrained by feeding, clothing and arming an extra 300,000 men, but it must be remembered that the empire was technologically even more backward than Europe of the Middle Ages. With primitive methods of agriculture, industrial production and transport it took very many more manhours than today to produce the food for rations, to weave the fabrics for uni-

forms, to hammer out the arms and armour and to transport all this material by barge and wagon to the frontiers. Taxation had to be enormously increased, and to assess and collect the increased taxes, the civil service had to be expanded, thus increasing the taxation load again.

The heavy burden of taxation was probably the root cause of the economic decline of the empire. Marginal lands, which could not yield a profit to the landlord over and above the taxes, ceased to be cultivated. The population seems also to have shrunk. This is a highly disputable point, but there are distinct signs of a chronic shortage of agricultural manpower, notably the reluctance of landlords to surrender their tenants as recruits, the legislation tying tenants to their farms, the constant attempts of landlords to filch tenants from their neighbours, and the large-scale settlement of barbarians on the land. The shortage was not due to a flight from the land to the towns—the movement was rather in the opposite direction. It was exacerbated by the demands of conscription, but it is difficult to resist the suggestion that the peasant population failed to maintain its numbers. The decline in the cultivated area, though not primarily due to manpower shortage, implies that the rural population did decline. The reason for this was that the peasantry, after paying their taxes, and the tenants their rent, did not retain enough food to rear large families, and many died of malnutrition or of actual starvation in bad seasons or after enemy devastations.

Ideally speaking the empire could of course have reduced the economic burden by rigid efficiency and drastic pruning of superfluities. It maintained large numbers of idle or nominal soldiers and sinecurist civil servants. According to old custom it fed 120,000 citizens of Rome, and added to these 80,000 citizens of Constantinople. These were a direct burden on the treasury. It also tolerated, and indeed encouraged, the growth of other classes of idle mouths, notably the clergy. Paganism had cost very little, its priests, except in Egypt, receiving no remuneration except portions of sacrifices. The churches, with their many thousands of clergy, maintained from agricultural rents and first fruits, constituted a new and substantial burden on the economy. The emperors moreover did nothing to curb the growth of the official aristocracy in numbers and wealth, and thus tolerated and encouraged the increase of another unproductive class.

The basic cause of the economic decline of the empire was in fact the increasing number of (economically speaking) idle mouths—senators with their vast households, decurions, civil servants, lawyers, soldiers, clergy, citizens of the capitals—as compared with the number of producers. The resultant burden of taxation and rents proved too much for the peasantry, who slowly dwindled in numbers.

It has been argued that the empire was weakened by the decay of its trade and industry. It is in fact very doubtful if trade and industry did decay; the production and distribution of high-grade and luxury goods for the rich certainly continued to flourish down to the sixth century, and the bulk of industrial and commercial activity had probably always been devoted to such goods. In any event industry and trade had at all times made so small a contribution to the national income that their decay, if it did occur, was economically unimportant.

This economic pressure was, it must be remembered, as severe in the eastern as in the western parts. The east maintained as large an army and a civil service, and had an even larger and richer body of clergy, if a less wealthy aristocracy, than the west. Its rate of taxation was very high, its marginal lands fell out of cultivation, and its population probably sank. But it had greater reserves of agricultural wealth and manpower on which to draw.

No one who reads the scanty records of the collapse of the western empire can fail to be struck by the apathy of the Roman population from the highest to the lowest. The only instance of concerted self help by the provincials is the action of the cities of Britain and Armorica in 408, when, failing to receive aid from the usurper Constantine, they organized their own defence against the barbarians, with the subsequent approval of Honorius. In 471–75 Sidonius Apollinaris, the bishop of their city, inspired the Arverni to defend themselves against the Visigoths. In 532 Pudentius raised his province of Tripolitania against the Vandals and, with the aid of a small imperial force, ejected them. In 546 Tullianus, a landlord of Lucania and Bruttium, organized a large body of peasants, which assisted the imperial forces against Totila. These are the only resistance movements of which we know. Elsewhere the upper classes either fled—there is ample evidence for Spain in 409, when the barbarians first broke in, and for the African provinces in 437 and 442, when the Vandals invaded them—or stayed put and collaborated with the barbarian kings. Not that they were active traitors, with one or two notorious exceptions, but they passively accepted their lot. They were very pleased in Africa and Italy when Justinian's armies arrived, but they did very little to help them.

The lower classes were just as inert. Townsmen would generally man the walls, but their object was to avoid a sack, and if guaranteed security they would usually surrender. Peasants, like their betters, sometimes fled in panic, but more often accepted their fate passively. They would fight if given a lead, as by Tullianus, but they would fight on either side. Totila subsequently ordered the landlords under his control to recall their peasants from Tullianus' force, and they meekly obeyed. Later Totila raised his own force of Italian peasants and they fought their fellow-citizens under Tullianus in bloody battles. Among the lower classes again there is very little evidence of active co-operation with the barbarians. In fact only one case is known; in 376 some Thracian miners joined the Goths and guided them to rich villas where stores of food were available. Having recently been recalled to their work from agriculture, they may have had a special grievance. It is alleged by Salvian that some peasants in Gaul fled to the barbarians to escape the oppression of landlords and tax collectors; this is no doubt true, but Salvian is a biased witness and perhaps exaggerates.

This apathy was not peculiar to the western parts; instances of self help are as rare in the east. Nor was it, so far as we know, anything new. There had been less occasion for civilian resistance to the enemy under the principate, when the armies on the whole held the invaders at the frontier, but no civilian action is recorded when a breakthrough did occur. For many centuries the provincials had been used to being protected by a professional army, and they had indeed, ever since the reign of Augustus, been prohibited by the *lex Iulia de vi* from bearing arms; this law was in force and more or less observed in the fifth century, and Justinian stiffened it by making the manufacture of arms a strict government monopoly. It was only on the rarest occasions that the government appealed to the civil population (including slaves) to take up arms to defend the empire; in 406 when Radagaesus with his horde had broken into Italy, the government appealed for volunteers "for love of peace and country," and in 440, when Gaiseric was threatening to invade Italy, it authorized the provincials to arm themselves to resist Vandal landing parties. It is not known whether either appeal was fruitful; in earlier crises Augustus and Marcus Aurelius had been obliged to apply conscription in Italy.

The general attitude of the provincials to the empire was, and always had been, passive. This is well illustrated under the principate by such panegyrics on the Roman empire as that of Aelius Aristides, and by the provincial cult of Rome and Augustus. Provincials were profoundly grateful to the empire for protecting them from the barbarians and maintaining internal security, and thus enabling them to enjoy and develop the amenities of civilized life in peace. But they felt no active loyalty, no obligation to help the emperor in his task. He was a god, whom they delighted to worship, but who needed no aid from his mortal subjects.

It has been argued that the regimentation of the population into hereditary castes led to inertia and discontent. It is true that many members of the classes affected tried to evade their hereditary obligations, but this does not prove that all were discontented. In any society, however free, most people are content to carry on in their parents' vocation, and it is only an enterprising few who strike out a new line and rise in the social scale. So far as we can tell the enterprising few in the later Roman empire normally succeeded in flouting or evading the law, which was very inefficiently enforced. The extent and the rigidity of the caste system have in any case been exaggerated, and it was, it may be noted, common to both east and west.

There was undoubtedly a decline in public spirit in the later Roman empire, both in the east and in the west. Under the principate there had existed a strong sense of civic patriotism among the gentry, and they had given freely of their time and money not only to improve the amenities of their cities, but to perform many administrative tasks, such as collecting the taxes and levying recruits, delegated to the cities by the imperial government. From the third century onwards this civic patriotism faded, and the imperial government had to rely more and more on its own administrators and civil servants. Under the principate the service of the state had been regarded as a high duty, incumbent on the imperial aristocracy, and on the whole, the government service being small and select, high standards were maintained. Under the later empire the old pagan idea of public service waned and the church taught good Christians to regard the imperial service as dirty work, if not sinful, while the ranks of the administration were greatly expanded and its quality inevitably diluted. Hence the growth of corruption and extortion, leading to popular discontent and waste of the limited resources of the empire. Over a wider field the teaching of the church that salvation was only to be found in the world to come and that the things of this world did not matter may have encouraged apathy and defeatism.

It must however be emphasized that the eastern empire shared to the full these various weaknesses, economic, social and moral, and that it nevertheless suvived for centuries as a great power. It was the increasing pressure of the barbarians, concentrated on the weaker western half of the empire, that caused the collapse.

SOLOMON KATZ (1909–   ) is Provost at the
University of Washington. His *Decline of Rome and
the Rise of Mediaeval Europe* offers a necessary
corrective to the mistaken notion that the fall of Rome
entailed the end of Roman civilization and that it
was a historical tragedy from which man has never
recovered. The final chapter is printed below.*

Solomon Katz

The Roman Legacy

The story of the rise and decline of
Rome has stirred the imagination of
mankind. In the thousand years of her
history Rome, originally a small farming community, had emerged first as
master of Italy and finally as ruler of
the western world. Her people had con-
solidated the Empire under the Roman
peace and buttressed it for centuries by
an efficient system of administration and
defense. Latin culture had been modified
as a result of exposure to intellectual and
artistic crosscurrents from the Graeco-
Oriental parts of the Empire, and out of
an amalgam of Oriental, Greek, and
Roman elements the Romans had created
a civilization of high order. The Roman
achievement was magnificent; the Roman
failure to meet the challenge presented
by new experiences and to solve the
problems posed by fresh responsibilities
was disastrous.

By A.D. 600 peace and unity were
shattered and the Roman Empire had
disintegrated. In the four centuries from
Marcus Aurelius to Justinian the Empire experienced civil war and anarchy,
barbarian invasions, and political and
economic crises. The Western Empire
ceased to exist, and upon its territories
the Germanic peoples created their
kingdoms. Eastern Roman emperors
still ruled from their capital at Constantinople, but over a greatly shrunken

* From Solomon Katz, *The Decline of Rome and the Rise of Mediaeval Europe*
(Ithaca, N.Y., 1955), 138–150. Reprinted by permission of the Cornell University Press.

empire. The physical decline of Rome was accompanied by a deterioration of her civilization as the ancient structure of thought weakened. The Roman gods, who had been closely identified with Roman civilization and with the state itself, were vanquished by Christianity, whose victory heralded a new epoch.

Confronted by all the profound material and spiritual changes which constitute the phenomenon described as the decline of the Roman Empire, one may well ask not why that empire declined, but rather how it was able to endure for so long. There were weaknesses in the Empire, as we have seen, but there were obviously also enormous reserves of strength. The unity which Rome imposed upon the Mediterranean world and the administrative system and the law which held the Empire together enabled her to resist for a long time the forces of disintegration. These institutions which served Rome so well endured as an important part of the Roman legacy. Roman civilization as a whole was greatly altered, but it survived the crises of the Later Empire and lived on as an integral element of mediaeval and modern civilization. Rome's triumphs and successes were canceled by her failure, but what she accomplished in diverse areas of endeavor was not lost. In the long perspective of history the survival of Roman civilization, the heritage which generation after generation has accepted, is perhaps more significant than the decline of Rome.

Rome's genius was essentially practical, and it was pre-eminently in the domain of administration that the Roman legacy was greatest. The Greeks had failed to achieve political unity and had exhausted their strength in inter-state warfare; the Romans, on the contrary, succeeded in building a world-state. By force, diplomacy, and sometimes by chicanery—one may not gloss over the story—the Romans unified the ancient world. For a congeries of antagonistic and mutually warring states Rome substituted the *Pax Romana,* safeguarded by an army, but secured even more by law and by a variety of administrative devices fairly and efficiently applied. The solidly founded political system which Rome extended over her vast empire was the institutional heritage which she bequeathed to later ages.

To the Eastern Roman Empire, which continued Rome's rule over a reduced area, to the barbarian states which took the place of the Western Roman Empire, and to the Christian church, Rome handed on the practices of government. The Eastern Roman emperors who ruled in almost unbroken sequence until the fall of Constantinople in 1453 accepted and maintained Roman principles of statecraft, and the German kings of western Europe likewise found in the Later Roman Empire a model for their absolute rule. They retained many of the features of the Roman administrative system: Roman imperial offices and perhaps municipal institutions, Roman titles and symbols of authority, the Roman system of public finances, Roman coin types, and above all, Roman law. From Rome too during these centuries the church received its basic organization, administration, and law. In the East and the West, church and state accepted the rich institutional heritage of Rome and thus perpetuated the ideals and traditions of the Roman state.

More important than any of these administrative practices was the Roman legacy in the realm of political ideals: common citizenship, political unity, a well-organized state living under law. Whatever the forms of government in their long history, whether monarchy or republic, the Principate of the Early Empire or the absolute, bureaucratic rule of the Later Empire, the Romans showed a virtual passion for these ideals. Long after the decline of the Empire they endured as Rome's major bequest to the world.

Roman citizenship had been extended to more and more of the inhabitants of the Empire until by the time of the emperor Caracalla (A.D. 212) it was almost universally held by free men. There were divisive forces which sundered East and West and separated the provinces from each other and from Italy itself. Nevertheless, in the great age of the Roman Empire a unified state was created out of peoples of different origins, and within the broad area of imperial unity local diversities of language, religion, customs, and institutions were tolerated. This was the achievement praised in the days of Rome's greatness by the Greek orator Aelius Aristides: "You have made the name of Rome no longer that of a city but of an entire people." It impressed the Christian poet Prudentius and his pagan and Christian contemporaries even in the period when Rome was in manifest decline: "A common law made them equals and bound them by a single name, bringing the conquered into bonds of brotherhood. We live in countries the most diverse like fellow-citizens of the same blood dwelling within the single ramparts of their native city and all united in an ancestral home."[1]

1 Prudentius, *A Reply to Symmachus*, II, 608–612; tr. by H. J. Thomson, *Prudentius* (Loeb Classical Library; Cambridge, Mass., 1953), II, 55.

The ideal of a common citizenship in a unified world was cherished centuries after it had passed out of the realm of practical politics. Although a single Roman Empire was replaced by separate German kingdoms in the West and by an Eastern Roman Empire in Constantinople, men clung tenaciously to their belief in the eternity of the Roman Empire. Long after the living memory of Rome's centralized rule was lost, and when, in fact, the growth of feudalism made such rule impossible, the ideal continued to have an irresistible appeal. The coronation of Charlemagne as Holy Roman Emperor in 800 and of Otto the Great in 962 are concrete manifestations of the persistent conviction that the Roman Empire had never perished and that imperial might had not decayed but had been transferred to other monarchs. However slight may have been the actual strength of the Holy Roman Empire in its history of a thousand years, it was a witness to the evocative power of Rome's name. So, too, the mediaeval ideal of a *Respublica Christiana*, a commonwealth represented by the church, was essentially the Roman tradition of universality modified by Christian thought.

The Roman law, the instrument and the symbol of her unity, was Rome's greatest achievement. The acceptance of this legacy by the Middle Ages gave both church and state a basis for their own systems of law and helped to civilize Europe by spreading widely the principles of equity and humanity which were embodied in the structure of the law. Roman law did not share the fate of the Empire. The barbarian conquerors retained both Roman law and law courts for their Roman subjects, and for their fellow Germans they harmonized Roman law and legal concepts with their own law and customs. In the Eastern Roman Empire, Roman law and legal theory, as crystallized in Justinian's great codification, remained in force for almost a thousand years. In the East and West during the Middle Ages the church erected canon law, its own legal system, upon Roman foundations.

Thus Roman law remained a vital force in the centuries after the decline of the Empire. Then at the end of the eleventh century interest in its principles was rekindled by the study of Justinian's *Corpus Iuris Civilis* at Bologna in Italy, and before long the law became a major subject of study in the universities of Europe. By the sixteenth century Roman law was increasingly applied in the European courts of law, and it served as the basis for the legal systems of the states of continental Europe and their overseas colonies. It still performs its ancient mission of binding together disparate peoples, for a large part of the Western world employs Roman law today. Even where legal systems, such as the common law of the English-speaking peoples, are not Roman in origin, many of their fundamental concepts are derived from Roman law and the very terms used to describe them are of Latin origin. Property, contract, agent, testament, judge, jury, crime: the terms and the legal and juridical concepts which they denominate are Roman.

Through its application Roman law has exercised a continuous influence upon the development of the law of the western world, but the underlying concepts of Roman law have equally influenced jurisprudence, philosophy, and politics.... [F]rom the time of Rome's earliest legal code, the Twelve Tables (c. 443 B.C.), the harshness of the law was steadily modified.

Under the impact first of Stoic philosophy and then of Christianity a greater emphasis was placed upon human rights and social justice, and the law became ever more enlightened. When the Roman jurists broadened their understanding of civil law to something like a "law of nations" and eventually to a kind of "natural law," they forged the link which binds Graeco-Roman and modern concepts of the rights and duties of the individual.

It is, however, not only in administration and law that the vitality of the Roman institutional heritage is apparent. The large estates or villas of the Later Empire, which were cultivated by half-free *coloni,* continued into the Middle Ages, and by a fusion of Roman and German elements became the manorial system of that period. Similarly the late Roman system of holding land under the protection of a strong landlord influenced feudal methods of land tenure in mediaeval Europe. Nor did the instruments by which Rome long maintained a flourishing urban life die. Even in the darkest period of the Middle Ages many Roman roads, although neglected, continued to be used. While Roman cities became impoverished and shrank in area and population, the more important ones never disappeared, but survived at least as centers of ecclesiastical administration and for such trade as existed. Today, fifteen hundred years after the end of the Western Empire, the traveler in Europe moves along the routes of ancient Roman roads and visits cities which have had a continuous history from antiquity to the present moment.

To Rome's practical skill as administrator and lawgiver we owe the preservation and dissemination of classical culture, for it was within the frame of institutions which they created that the Romans fashioned their culture by a synthesis of Greek, Oriental, and Roman elements. But for these institutions Roman culture and with it much of Greek culture might not have survived.

Rome's native culture had been changed as a result of her contacts with the Greeks of southern Italy and Sicily and eventually by her acquisition of the Greek East. The culture of her new subjects in the eastern provinces was Greek, and Roman culture itself was soon so thoroughly permeated with Hellenic elements that it may more accurately be described as Graeco-Roman. Roman schools began to offer a system of education which was essentially Greek. Greek literature, philosophy, and rhetoric were eagerly studied at Rome and became acknowledged models for Roman writers. Most of the literary forms employed by Roman authors, much of their imagery and symbolism, their mythology, the very meters of their poetry, were borrowed from the Greeks. Roman artists and architects adapted Greek canons and techniques of art and architecture to their own needs and made them an integral part of the Roman heritage to western civilization. By unifying and by Romanizing the ancient world the Romans enabled their culture, of which the Greek element was so important a part, to spread throughout the Mediterranean basin and western Europe. Strong enough to outlast the collapse of the Empire, Graeco-Roman civilization was preserved by the new states of western Europe, the Eastern Roman Empire, and the church.

To the civilization which they developed the Romans contributed many distinctively Roman elements. Chief among these was the Latin language, which gradually replaced the native tongues of Rome's subjects in the western half of the Empire and which in time the German conquerors adopted as their own language of administration and literature. It was in Latin that the western church Fathers wrote; it was into Latin that St. Jerome translated the Bible; it was in Latin that for centuries poets, historians, and theologians wrote their works. The church in the West used Latin for its ritual and for its official documents, as it does even today. As the language of literature, learning, and law during the Middle Ages, Latin was in effect an international language which recognized no frontiers in the West. In contrast, therefore, to all the centrifugal forces of the period, Latin served as a bond of unity.

For a thousand years after the disintegration of the Empire, Latin survived as the leading, and for much of that time the only, language of literature. For learning and law it was supreme until the seventeenth and eighteenth centuries. Although Latin has been superseded by the modern languages for most scholarly and scientific purposes outside the church, it remains today an important part of the school curriculum wherever the European educational tradition prevails. Thus the key to the treasures of Latin literature has been handed down from generation to generation.

Even when Latin was no longer a regular means of communication, its influence remained strong. It was out of the popular or Vulgar Latin spoken by the common people of the Roman Empire that the Romance languages—Italian, French, Spanish, Portuguese, and

Roumanian—gradually came into being during the Middle Ages. Moreover, such non-Latin languages as English contain a high proportion of words derived from Latin; in fact, it has been estimated that from half to two-thirds of the words commonly employed in English are of Latin origin. To Latin the English-speaking peoples owe a large part of their philosophic and scientific vocabulary as well as many of the words by which they denote political, social, and economic institutions. The very scripts used in mediaeval manuscripts were Roman in origin, and the Roman alphabet itself was adopted by the Romance, Celtic, and Germanic languages, several of the Slavic tongues, and by other languages such as Hungarian, Finnish, and Turkish. Clearly the Latin language is one of the greatest and most enduring of Rome's many bequests to western civilization.

For nearly two thousand years men have regarded Latin literature as a very precious part of their inheritance from ancient Rome. Despite their fears that they might be corrupted by them, the church Fathers of the early centuries read and studied Latin authors and by their own example showed how classical literature might be put to Christian uses. Even in the darkest period of the Middle Ages the ancient authors were not forgotten. In the monasteries, the centers of learning at that time, the monks copied and preserved the texts of classical authors, while in the newly established states of western Europe, Germanic kings were often active patrons of Latin letters. Throughout the Middle Ages the literature of ancient Rome remained a fundamental part of the course of study in the schools. When in the later **Middle Ages** the universities were

founded, Latin literature was one of the staples of instruction. Either in its own right or by helping to shape the vernacular literature which eventually superseded it, Latin literature remained a vital force throughout the mediaeval period. With the Renaissance there came not a rebirth but an intensification of interest in a literature which had suffered vicissitudes but whose study had never been abandoned. Latin literature is read today by fewer people than in the past. It is, however, so firmly embedded in the western cultural tradition that it still wields a dominating influence. Scarcely a branch or genre of writing in the modern world can be named which has not to some extent been molded by the work of a Roman author. Cicero helped to fashion the language and thought of the western world, Seneca the philosophy and tragedy, Plautus and Terence the comedy, Virgil and Horace the poetry, Ovid the mythology.

The Roman legacy in architecture and art has been equally rich. Not only was Roman architecture a prime factor in the development of the ecclesiastical architecture of the Middle Ages, but it largely determined the plan of mediaeval secular buildings. The arch, the dome, and the vault—forms of construction which the Romans either developed out of their own creative genius or else made peculiarly their own—have had a continuous life in the East and the West from ancient times to our day. In painting, sculpture and the minor arts, too, Roman standards of craftsmanship and canons of taste have contributed immensely to the establishment of an artistic tradition in western civilization.

However great the Roman institutional and cultural heritage may be, it is overshadowed by one contribution which the Empire, by the very fact of its existence, made to western civilization. It was in the Roman Empire that Christianity came into being and finally won supremacy. The *Pax Romana*, the peace which Rome gave to the ancient world, facilitated the spread of Christianity and made possible the translation into reality of the ideal of a universal religion. When the political unity of the Roman world was destroyed, a new spiritual unity, represented by the church, took its place and served as a binding force for the Middle Ages.

In its triumph the church did not reject the past, but built upon Roman foundations and within the frame furnished by the Roman Empire. From Rome the church inherited its institutions, its organization, its administrative system, and its law. From Rome the church in the West received the Latin language, a potent instrument of unity. Latin literature and learning gave a higher intellectual quality to Christianity, and Roman art furnished the basic forms for Christian art. By accepting and making its own this rich Roman heritage, the church built a bridge between the ancient world and the modern.

Western civilization rests upon Greek, Roman, and Hebrew-Christian foundations. To Rome we owe an incalculable debt for building a great civilization in which was incorporated and preserved the Graeco-Oriental culture which she herself inherited and for providing a setting into which Christianity, her own heir, could come into being. For more than two thousand years the western world has been taught and inspired by Rome. Deeply rooted in western civilization, Roman ideals and practices still bear witness to the magnificent achievement of Eternal Rome.

Suggestions for Further Reading

Any reading about the decline of Rome would naturally include a sampling of Edward Gibbon's *History of the Decline and Fall of the Roman Empire.* The best edition of Gibbon is by J. B. Bury (7 vols., London, 1896–1900). A handy abridgment of Gibbon was made by D. M. Low (London, 1960), who has also written the standard biography, *Edward Gibbon* (London, 1937). The *Memoirs* of Gibbon, originally edited by his friend Lord Sheffield and often called the *Autobiography*, explain Gibbon's choice of his subject and provide a charming picture of the eighteenth-century mind; see D. A. Saunders' edition of the *Autobiography* (New York, 1961). A series of essays surveying Gibbon's problem at the distance of two centuries is edited by Lynn White, Jr.: *The Transformation of the Roman World* (Berkeley and Los Angeles, 1966).

There are several comprehensive modern histories of the later Empire. Bury's *History of the Later Roman Empire* has been reprinted by Dover Publications, Inc. (New York, 1958). The basic work for reference is now A. H. M. Jones's *The Later Roman Empire, 284–602* (Oxford, 1964); his *The Decline of the Ancient World* (New York, 1966) is an abridgment of the former work. On the same large scale is Ernst Stein, *Histoire du Bas-empire* (vol. I, Paris, 1959; vol. II, 1949; the first volume appeared in German in 1928).

Among more specialized studies is Ferdinand Lot, *The End of the Ancient World and the Beginnings of the Middle Ages* (New York, 1931; reprinted by Harper Torchbooks, 1961). The reprint has an introduction by Glanville Downey, one of our senior Byzantine historians, who also supplies an excellent annotated bibliography. Focusing on the same area are W. C. Bark, *Origins of the Medieval World* (Stanford, 1958), and Joseph Vogt, *The Decline of Rome* (London, 1968). Santo Mazzarino's *The End of the Ancient World* (New York, 1966) is a set of essays rather than a consecutive treatment of the theme. Shorter general works are R. F. Arragon, *The Transition from the Ancient to the Medieval World* (New York, 1936) and Richard Haywood, *The Myth of Rome's Fall* (New York, 1958). The latter's thesis is that the fall was not inevitable or due to any single major cause: thus there is no "lesson" for the modern world in the event. An overall discussion of the fall is the lecture by A. H. M. Jones, "The Decline and Fall of the Roman Empire," *History,* 40 (1955), 209–226.

The third century, when one emperor followed another through several chaotic decades, was the critical period for the Empire. Recent studies (mainly in German) have concentrated to some degree on administrative problems. See G. Walser, "Zu den Ursachen der Reichskrise im dritten nachchristlichen Jahrhundert," *Schweizer Beiträge zur allgemeinen Geschichte,* 18–19 (1960–1961), 142–161; J. Moreau, "Krise und Verfall: das dritte Jahrhundert n. Chr. als historisches Problem," *Heidelberger Jahrbuch,* 5 (1961), 128–142. Several papers by the Hungarian scholar Andreas Alföldi were reprinted as *Studien zur Geschichte der Weltkrise des 3. Jahrhunderts nach Chr.* (Darmstadt, 1967). G. Walser and T. Pekáry have issued a survey of work on this period since 1939, arranged according to the chapter titles of vol. XI of the Cambridge Ancient History: *Die Krise des römischen Reiches* (Berlin, 1962). A similar work with a narrative and discussion of historical problems is R. Rémondon's *La Crise de l'Empire romain de Marc-Aurèle à Anastase* (Paris, 1964).

A collection of views was made in an interesting study by L. Stecchini, "The Historical Problem of the Fall of Rome," *Journal of General Education*, 5 (1950–1951), 57–88. After an introductory discussion he reprints selections in translation from Maschkin, a Marxist historian, A. Piganiol, and Max Weber. The selection by Piganiol comes from his *L'Empire chrétien* (Paris, 1947), where he reviews many theories and concludes that the Empire was "assassinated." This conclusion is reinforced by A. R. Hands, "The Fall of the Roman Empire in the West: A Case of Suicide or *Force Majeure*?", *Greece & Rome*, ser. 2, 10 (1963), 153–168; he emphasizes the external causes for the fall. Max Weber's economic explanation—that the modest "house-economy" of the Middle Ages could not sustain the industrial productivity of disciplined masses of slaves—can be found in his *General Economic History* (New York, 1927); his basic statements were made in his *Die römische Agrargeschichte* (Stuttgart, 1891).

Others have joined Weber in arguing for one or another kind of economic causation. "Rome's Fall Reconsidered," an article by V. Simkhovitch in *Political Science Quarterly*, 31 (1916), 201–243, suggests that regressive methods of cultivation had depleted the soil of Italy and had physically enfeebled the Empire. This position was accepted in principle by Ellsworth Huntington in such books as *Civilization and Climate* (3d ed.; New York, 1924) and *The Pulse of Progress* (New York, 1926). See further W. L. Westermann, "The Economic Basis of the Decline of Ancient Culture," *American Historical Review*, 20 (1914–1915), 723–743; L. C. West, "The Economic Collapse of the Roman Empire," *Classical Journal*, 28 (1932–1933), 96–106.

Tenney Frank's article on the racial composition of the Empire was strongly criticized by Mary L. Gordon, "The Nationality of Slaves under the Early Roman Empire," *Journal of Roman Studies*, 14 (1924), 93–111. She suggests that Greek names of slaves may have been arbitrarily bestowed by slave-traders and may not prove that those so named were in fact Greeks or Easterners. Another thesis about the changing personnel of the Empire is that of Otto Seeck. In his massive study of the decline of the ancient world, he maintained that the destruction of the better people (the "Ausrottung der Besten") by the Emperors stripped the Empire of its creative citizens: see his *Geschichte des Untergangs der antiken Welt* (vol. I, Stuttgart, 1921, 269–307). Hugh Last of Oxford gave at least tentative support to Seeck in a letter to Norman Baynes, *Journal of Roman Studies*, 37 (1947), 152–156.

Boak's researches on population may be supplemented by J. C. Russell, *Late Ancient and Medieval Population, Transactions of the American Philosophical Society*, new series, 48.3 (Philadelphia, 1958). Disease must have taken its toll from the population, as is argued by W. H. S. Jones, *Malaria, a Neglected Factor in the History of Greece and Rome* (Cambridge, 1907); see further J. F. Gilliam, "The Plague under Marcus Aurelius," *American Journal of Philology*, 82 (1961), 225–251: Gilliam does not consider the plague a major cause of the decline. Another recent study on population is F. G. Maier, "Römische Bevölkerungsgeschichte und Inschriftenstatistik," *Historia*, 2 (1953–1954), 318–351.

Political causes for the fall (discussed by Walbank in this booklet) have been examined by several scholars. W. E. Heitland, *The Roman Fate* (Cambridge, 1922), argues that Rome sealed her doom by not allowing popular will to be sufficiently expressed; see further his pamphlets *Iterum, Last Words on the Roman Municipalities*, and *Repetita* (Cambridge, 1925, 1928, 1930). An interesting line is pursued by G. R. Monks, "The Administration of the Privy Purse: An Inquiry into Official Corruption and the Fall of the Roman Empire," *Speculum*, 32 (1957),

748–779. The often-sponsored theory of inevitable ruin is attacked by J. J. Saunders, "The Debate on the Fall of Rome," *History*, 48 (1963), 1–17. Freya Stark, in her *Rome on the Euphrates* (London, 1966), indicts Roman imperialism for making war with eastern nations rather than trying to establish lasting commercial relations between East and West.

Some of the larger implications of the fall of Rome are treated by W. Rehm, *Der Untergang Roms im abendländischen Denken* (Leipzig, 1930), where he surveys the changing attitudes toward the problem of decline from antiquity to the nineteenth century. See also H. Werner, *Der Untergang Roms: Studien zum Dekadenz-problem in der antiken Geistesgeschichte* (Stuttgart, 1939). And for the further influence of Rome on Europe, see Cyril Bailey, ed., *The Legacy of Rome* (Oxford, 1923).

These writings, along with the excerpts reprinted in the text, nearly all refer to much other literature, to which the reader can find his way without a guide.